The BEAT Coaching System

By Shawn Carson
and
Sarah Carson

Table of Contents

Foreword
Michael Watson

Have you ever wanted to be different than you are? We all have. Perhaps it's a certain quality or characteristic that we wish we could develop. Maybe we'd like to be a little more evolved in some particular way. Maybe we want some special skills. Or maybe we're seeking a complete overhaul ... a re-invention. Whether you're looking for a way to change your golf score or to change your life... This book is for you.

This book is a part of a process... It is a part of a journey, your journey. And even though I don't know what set you on this path or all the details that led up to you selecting this title, I think I can make a few assumptions about you just because you decided to read it. You have a curious mind, and you're interested in exploring. You're "on the road to find out".

And I'm even willing to guess that this isn't the first time you've picked up a book with the hope of discovering something that you could actually use to make a big difference in your life. Maybe you're a relative newcomer to the domain of coaching, or changework, or whatever you like to call this sort of thing. Or maybe you've already studied a great deal and are still intrigued by new understandings and nuances that can enrich your earlier learning.

So although I don't know where you've come from or where you're headed, I know that you're in the right place with this book.

I've been on my journey for six decades. And I spent the first three getting ready. I was always on a quest. By the time I was thirty, the road to ready had led me through religion and meditation, psychedelics, encounter groups, EST seminars; all in pursuit of some mystical transcendent "OKness" that would somehow make all the difference. And it was groovy for a while.

Then I started to grow up. One day more than thirty years ago my practical nature (finally) surfaced and I realized that my quest for The Great Nebulous had become more specific. The question changed, and I started wondering: "How can people create the lives that they really want to have?"

Perhaps one of the biggest limitations of traditional approaches to change is that the focus is generally on the idea that something is wrong and change is necessary. There's some presenting problem or limitation to be overcome. There's a sense of urgency. And often there is some serious soul-searching involved, sensitive memories to be exposed and explored. It's an other-than-happy process with an emphasis on fixing things that don't work.

Neuro Linguistic Programming has held my attention for the past three decades because it offers something different. It is a forward- looking approach that is devoted to the process of creation. Although it CAN be used to resolve problems, it doesn't have to wait for trouble to come along. It simply asks, "What do you want to create today?" And sets about the business of doing that.
NLP recognizes that behavior occurs within the context of states, and that the key to succeeding at anything has to do with being in a state that supports success. In other words, "Get your head in the right place and you can change your life."

John Grinder, co-creator of NLP once said that what was required to create change was congruity and a ritual. As I understand it, he was referring to an earnest intention and a procedure that you can use to access the peak states involved in generating and integrating the new behaviors, or attitudes, or identities, or whatever you want.

At its heart, NLP is about modeling. It is a study of the nuances and components of experience. And through the years of its development a lot of distinctions have been made. There are representations and submodalities and metaprograms and language patterns and more and more until the average end-user is overwhelmed with the complexity of its presentation. And then there are numerous patterns and techniques to choose between. And as a system, it becomes unwieldy for personal use by anyone other than the most skillful practitioners.

The paradox is that the purpose of all this modeling has been to seek the essence of something and to distill it for ease of replication. So modeling itself needs to be remodeled or refashioned in a way that shakes off some of its complications by resynthesizing the elements involved. The primary consideration is, how to access the necessary states and give them expression in our bodies, in our emotions, in our awareness and in our thoughts.
So isn't it nice to know that finally, the Carsons have written a book that accomplishes that purpose nicely! This is real NLP without any pre-requisites. Everything you need to know to understand and use it is right here in this straight-forward approach that you can begin to use immediately.

I first heard of the BEAT Pattern at a professional gathering of Hypnotherapists when Sarah Carson shared the basics of it in a 1 hour presentation. I was delighted with the elegance and clarity of her presentation, the impressive simplicity of the pattern itself, and the richness of the experience that it offered. Mentally, I filed it away as something that I might want to use from time to time.

But what really impressed me was that over the course of the next few weeks and months, I found myself using it time and time again with clients I work with in my own practice. I presented it to a group myself, and then I invited Sarah to be a guest in a monthly mentoring program that I facilitate via teleconference. It seemed like there was no end to its usefulness and I could apply it in every imaginable context.

That was a year ago, and my enthusiasm for the BEAT is as strong as ever. I keep finding more and more ways to employ and enjoy this wonderful process. And apparently the same has been true for the authors who have crafted into A COMPLETE SYSTEM of change.

In these pages they will share with you a tool kit that you can use for accessing powerful peak states to creating rich experiences for yourself. At will. In just 4 steps! They'll show you how to use it for problem solving and for self-creation. For exploration and discovery. You'll find applications for sports enhancement, meditation, social contexts, and others as you begin to discover your own variations and uses for it.

I wonder if you realized what you were getting into when you opened this book. Because you're going to get much more that you bargained for. The material presented here will give you what you need to create the rich, fulfilling life that you want. Use it in all contexts, from improving your performance in business, changing personal habits, improving your relationships, and even playing a better game of golf! The applications are virtually unlimited.

We're all on some kind of a journey or other. The BEAT Coaching System is a vehicle. This book is your ticket to ride. It extends an invitation to your future.

Introduction

Earlier books within our NLP Mastery Series have focused on one particular "pattern" from NLP. An NLP pattern is a sequence of "steps" that a coach asks a client to take in order to transform a problem or generate a solution. Each step could be a physical action by the client (for example, the coach might ask the client to "move here" or "sit in this chair") or a physical action by the coach (for example, touching a client's shoulder in order to "anchor" a particular state). However, more often than not, it is a mental task—a "thought" by the client (for example, the coach might ask the client to "see yourself on a movie screen...").

This book is a little bit different because we're presenting a complete system of change, a complete system of coaching, and a complete system of self-mastery. The reason the BEAT Coaching System is far more than just another NLP pattern is that it gives you complete control over all the elements of your state and all the elements of your experience in the "now" in any context. Once you understand and master the BEAT Coaching System, you will be in total control of yourself.

We have been able to build the system by separating out each element of current experience, optimizing each one separately, and then recombining them into a peak performance state. You'll see what we mean as we begin to describe the system.

The NLP BEAT Coaching System has a very specific purpose—to allow you to step into a peak performance state whenever you wish.

As usual in our NLP Mastery Series, we will begin by describing the history and neuroscience of the BEAT System in Section 1. Some of our readers enjoy this background information and have complained when we publish books in the NLP Mastery Series without it. However, if you are of a more practical mindset and want to get right down to learning how to use the BEAT System with your coaching clients or with yourself to enter your peak states at will, you can safely pass over the chapters on the history and neuroscience if you so choose without missing a BEAT!

In Section 2, we will give you a thorough overview of the BEAT Coaching System. We will discuss each of the steps and give a brief transcript of a demonstration. We will discuss peak states and the principles of NLP anchoring. All of this should allow the reader to begin to build an understanding of an "idealized" form of the BEAT.

We will also go through each step of the BEAT Coaching System in more detail and describe variations that you can try. By going through the system in detail, practitioners will begin to understand some of the underlying structures and techniques of NLP that are embedded within the BEAT. This understanding will give practitioners the flexibility to apply NLP in a more generative way.

As the book progresses, we will add even more detail and more sophistication to the pattern. However, simply reading Section 2 will give you all the information you need in order to get started with the BEAT.

In Section 3, we will show you how to integrate the BEAT into your life to reach your goals and achieve your dreams.

In Section 4, we will talk about how to apply the BEAT in various situations, from coaching to self-coaching to business to mindfulness and meditation as well as several other contexts. This section will provide you with ready-made templates for applying the BEAT across several contexts and will also begin the process of integrating and generalizing what you have learned in the rest of the book.

About the BEAT

The BEAT Coaching System was developed by Shawn Carson of NLP and Hypnosis Training and the International Center for Positive Change and Hypnosis in New York City. It is a system that utilizes the NLP principles of spatial and kinesthetic "anchors" to create and control peak performance states. If you are not familiar with NLP anchoring, you can relax, as we will summarize this important NLP tool in a later chapter. However, the BEAT differs from standard anchoring patterns in that it does not simply seek to create an emotional response based upon the anchor, but also utilizes changes in physiology, sensory awareness, and internal representations as part of the anchoring process. This may sound complicated, but in fact the BEAT system is very easy to use and very easy to teach your clients once you understand it.

Although we will go through the BEAT System in detail in the book, hypnotists and coaching practitioners who want to use the BEAT with their clients should be aware that every client they deal with is unique. The unique personality of an individual may provide unique challenges in applying the BEAT. Throughout the book, we will seek to discuss variations and options regarding the system so as to encourage flexibility and experimentation on the part of the practitioner. Remember, NLP is "an attitude of wanton curiosity that leaves behind a trail of techniques," according to Richard Bandler, the cofounder of NLP. Holding this in mind, you can think of the BEAT System as simply another way to become curious about your client!

Controlling Peak States

As we have said, the BEAT System is all about accessing and controlling your peak states and those of your clients. Once you understand the BEAT, you will be able to access any and all peak states at will, and you will be able to amplify your peak states so they become even more powerful.

And when you are able to control your peak states—to access them at will and make them even more powerful—you will be able to achieve amazing things in your life. The person who is able to control her peak states is the top performer, the person who rises to the top of her profession, and the person who is most successful in life.

Now, you already know what a peak state is, or perhaps you know it when you see it. In Section 2, we will talk about what makes up a peak performance state, but right now let's work by example. Imagine a sportsman stepping up to take a shot—perhaps a golfer who is about to take a putt. You will notice that he engages in a particular ritual. These rituals may be similar within a certain sport, although each one is actually unique to the individual involved.

Watch the golfer step forward to take his shot. He will walk in a certain way, he will stand in a certain way, he will hold the golf club in a certain way, he may bend to remove a piece of grass from in front of his ball even if there is no piece of grass there. He may loosen his shoulders and perhaps take a practice swing. These movements represent rituals that allow him to step into his own peak state. The rituals act as signals to his nervous system that his peak "driving state" or "putting state" is required right then and there. Although all we see is his external behaviors, you can imagine that he is going through similar rituals internally, within his mind. On some level, he is doing the BEAT, even though he may not call it that.

We will go through all the aspects of the BEAT System first to make sure all the elements are in place. But once you have the BEAT System down, it will become an automatic ritual for you within a particular context that you can perform in a few seconds. It will become a signal to your nervous system to enter your own peak state. At that point, entering your peak state will become automatic for you.

Using Peak States

Of course, it is no use simply having a peak state—you need to *use* the state. To do this, you need to be able to select the correct peak state for a particular context, maintain the peak state in ways necessary to achieve your goal within that context, and reenter the peak state easily if and when you need to. This represents a "meta" level of using the BEAT, not just in the moment but throughout your life.

When you have this sort of control over your peak states, you will be able to achieve success in your life. The BEAT System gives you a specific and repeatable methodology to enter the peak state, keep yourself in the peak state, and reenter the peak state should you need to, for example, if you are thrown off your game by some external event. You see, the BEAT System only takes a second to do once it has been installed and conditioned; you can easily afford to invest one second to step into your peak state!

So all you have to do is begin to track your own state so that you know when you are in a less than optimal state, and then use the BEAT System to change your state whenever you want or need to.

Not only that, but you can create different BEAT Systems, associated with different peak states, for different contexts. So you can actually choose which peak state you want to be in, depending upon what you need in the specific context. You can have a peak state for playing a sport and a different peak state for being in a business meeting. You can have a peak state for being at a party and a different peak state for being with your family.

As you can probably tell, we get pretty excited when we talk about the BEAT! We could go on forever telling you how wonderful it is and how it will totally change your life when you're able to step into your peak state at will. But at some point we should actually tell you how the BEAT works, so let's move on to the first chapter!

Section 1:

Background and Neuroscience

Chapter 1: History of the BEAT Coaching System

John Overdurf's Mind Power and the Self-Coaching Pattern

In our school of NLP and HNLP (Humanistic Neuro Linguistic Psychology), we believe that lineage is very important. Your lineage refers to the chain of teachers that came before you. Richard Bandler and John Grinder, as well as Tad James, trained a number of master trainers before agreeing to go their separate ways. Two of these master trainers were John Overdurf and Julie Silverthorne.

One of the early products that John and Julie produced was a video called *Mind Power for Life*. This product was so old that it was only ever available on VHS and, as far as we know, is no longer in production. We were fortunate enough to get a copy of *Mind Power for Life* from John (he was giving them away once VHS was replaced by DVD!).

I watched the video and stored the Mind Power technique away in my mental vault of NLP techniques, but otherwise didn't really do anything with it at the time. However, unbeknownst to my conscious mind, my unconscious was busy considering and reconsidering the Mind Power pattern and "trying it on" in different contexts. I'm not sure exactly when, but one day it became obvious to me that anyone could easily and simply step into a peak state using a few powerful techniques from NLP and HNLP. At that moment, the hardest part about designing the system was coming up with the acronym B-E-A-T!

Having developed the system, all that remained was to test it. I use it extensively with my coaching clients, taught several workshops around it, and integrated it into our NLP Master Practitioner course. I also became obsessive about using it myself, for myself, in virtually every context I could think of, from business meetings to presentations to teaching to coaching to practicing martial arts to socializing. Based on my research, it seemed that the BEAT System could optimize my performance in any context, yet was simple enough to teach someone in ten minutes.

As my experimentation with the BEAT System continued, I refined it and added complementary techniques such as John Overdurf's Self-Coaching Method (which we describe in detail in Chapter 6).

For me, the most amazing thing about the BEAT Coaching System is how ubiquitous it is. When you understand the BEAT, you begin to see it everywhere, in all sorts of disciplines. We would go so far as to say that any discipline that seeks to optimize the human experience in the moment—to achieve peak states, if you will—always uses some version of the BEAT System.

For example, Tai Chi Chuan, the Chinese martial art, can be traced back to the tenth century. It includes instruction in how to use the body (B), internal energy (E), sensory awareness (A), and mental imagery or thoughts (T) during practice. The integration of these four elements—B-E-A-T—through the practice of Tai Chi Chuan leads to ideal states of performance.

The oldest reference I have been able to find to a discipline that specifically uses the BEAT format comes from the samurai classic *The Book of Five Rings*. This classic of samurai warfare was written in 1645 by Miyamoto Musashi, who was without any doubt the greatest samurai warrior ever. *The Book of Five Rings*—the number one book selection in the library of any budding samurai—contains a description of Musashi's fighting system and describes his own individual BEAT System (obviously it's not called the BEAT in Musashi's book!). We will describe Musashi's samurai BEAT in Chapter 22.

Despite the long and noble lineage of the BEAT System, it is not part of the classical NLP canon. You won't learn it in any practitioner course, or even master practitioner course, unless you study with one of our trainers or someone who has learned the BEAT directly or indirectly from us.

Having said this, for anyone versed in NLP, the BEAT System is recognizably a part of NLP. For example, it incorporates several classic NLP techniques, including spatial anchoring, kinesthetic anchoring, and auditory anchoring as well as chaining anchors. We also make use of internal representations and submodalities to make the system more powerful and effective.

Brief History of NLP

Richard Bandler and John Grinder developed Neuro Linguistic Programming, or NLP, in the 1970s. Bandler and Grinder modeled some of the best therapists who were practicing at that time—people like Virginia Satir, the leading exponent of family therapy; Fritz Perls, the founder of Gestalt therapy; and Milton Erickson, the father of modern hypnosis. By studying the patterns of these experts, Bandler and Grinder were able to discover the patterns of behavior and communication that were being used by these masters to achieve amazing results with their clients.

One of the principal tools developed as part of NLP is anchoring. Anchoring refers to the linking of an internal state to an external trigger. Anchors occur naturally all the time; for example, you and your life partner may have "your song." When you hear your song, perhaps it makes you feel romantic or sexy. Similarly, when you hear your national anthem being played, you might feel patriotic. And when you see your boss's face, perhaps you feel... Well, I don't know what you feel; it depends on you and your boss and the relationship the two of you have!

Anchoring is used in NLP by first associating your client into a particular state and then linking it to a certain touch, or a word said with a certain tonality, or even a facial expression or gesture. Anchoring is a key part of the BEAT, as you will see.

However, NLP is not just about techniques. Richard Bandler defined NLP as an "attitude of wanton experimentation that leaves behind a trail of techniques." According to this definition, NLP is an attitude, a way of dealing with people. If you see Richard Bandler at work, you will realize that he is intensely curious about the experience of his clients. He wants to understand how they do what they do, even when what they do is not working for them (i.e., when they have a "problem").

As far as Bandler is concerned, NLP patterns are simply a way of recording what a practitioner has done with a specific client so the practitioner can try the same steps with the next client. Although part of what was done with one client may be applicable to another client, Bandler recognizes that each client is a unique individual with a unique mind and a unique way of experiencing the world. Hence, flexibility is absolutely vital in dealing with clients, or indeed with yourself. This is the attitude that you should bring to learning and applying the BEAT in your own coaching practice or your own life.

The "Method"

If you have read our book on Deep Trance Identification (*Deep Trance Identification* by Shawn Carson and Jess Marion with John Overdurf), you'll know that we are big fans of the acting teacher Konstantin Stanislavski and his "method acting." This is because the art of stepping into a character for a play or movie using Stanislavski's method is virtually identical to stepping into your own future self—the person you want to become—using NLP. Stanislavski presents a set of techniques for doing this that are very applicable to life coaching and other change work.

Stanislavski's ideas are presented in his seminal works *An Actor Prepares* and *Building a Character*. These books are very dense, and unfortunately many people, including coaches and even actors, avoid them for this reason. Fortunately, there are several more simplified approaches that spring from Stanislavski's work. For example, there is an approach called TEAM that was developed by Laura Facciponti Bond from the University of North Carolina. The TEAM approach developed by Professor Bond is very similar to the BEAT System. Although I was not aware of the TEAM approach prior to developing the BEAT, once I learned about the TEAM approach, the parallels were obvious.

We will talk about using the BEAT System in the context of acting in Chapter 20.

Tree of Life

One of the principal tools we use in our school of coaching is based upon the Tree of Life from the Kabbalah. The Tree of Life is a wonderful model of human experience based upon ten points, or "Sephirot," of the Tree, which are linked by twenty-two "pathways."

We developed our Tree of Life coaching model several years after we developed the BEAT Coaching System.

As soon as we looked at the Tree of Life in the context of coaching, we realized that adjusting the lower triad (the lower three Sephirot) of the Tree to their ideal position produced the BEAT System.

You can refer to our upcoming book, *Tree of Life Coaching*, for a complete discussion of the relationship between the BEAT and the Tree of Life.

Chapter 2: Neuroscience of the BEAT System

The Mind and Body Are One System

Over the last thirty years, scientists have learned an enormous amount about the brain. They have been able to use fMRIs and other brain-scanning techniques to build an increasingly accurate picture of how the brain functions when performing certain tasks. Although neuroscience is in many ways still in its infancy, we know far more about how the brain, and the brain-body system, works than we ever have before.

As a result of this research, we know that the brain and the body act as a single system. When you even think about performing a physical action, your premotor cortex begins to respond as if you were actually taking that action. It's as if your body is preparing to take the action even before you've made a decision to do so. For example, when the brain reads a story that involves actions such as running or walking, the parts of the brain responsible for those actions light up. What this means is that thinking about something has a direct impact on your body.

This phenomenon is so pronounced that athletes who engage in mental practice are able to improve their performance to the same degree as athletes who actually practice. Several studies in this area have focused on basketball players (because it is very easy to measure the accuracy of free throws). These studies show that mental rehearsal can provide the same or better results in terms of improved performance as actual practice.

Similarly, when you read about an emotion, you begin to experience that emotion yourself. Not only does your physical-muscular body react to your thoughts, but your emotional body does as well.

Now, it is important to understand that this is not a one-way street. It is not simply that your muscular and emotional bodies respond to your thoughts. Your muscular body also responds to your emotions, and your emotions respond to your muscular body. Everything is connected in a web of cause and effect.

For example, research shows that simply walking with "happy feet" (i.e., with a lighthearted gait) makes you feel happier, while walking with a stooped or "depressed" gait makes you feel sadder.

Gestures can also affect your emotional state. For example, research shows that making wide, expansive gestures with your hands and arms makes you feel more confident and actually boosts the amount of testosterone in your system. Crossing your arms can make you feel more determined, and tensing your muscles gives you greater willpower.

Moving the palms of your hands toward you makes you more open to new information, while pushing your palms away allows you to focus on your own ideas.

We will be using these connections between the body, the mind, and the emotions when we build a BEAT System for each individual context.

Our Emotions

What are emotions? Are your emotions the sensations you feel inside your body when you are happy or sad, in love or angry? Or are emotions the labels that you put on these feelings—words like *happy*, *sad*, *love*, and *anger*?

It turns out that both of these answers are correct. In fact, emotions are the results of a complicated internal system designed to "set" your body and brain in the optimal way to achieve your goals, including the goal of survival.

You see, as you go through your day, your brain has to make decisions about how best to cope with what is going on around you. For example, suppose you have just eaten lunch. Your body moves into the "rest and digest" state, relaxing you and directing blood flow to your stomach to aid in digestion. Suddenly your brain sees something that it thinks is dangerous (a saber-toothed tiger, perhaps), and your brain now has to make a new decision about the priority of blood flow.

Before it makes these physical changes, your brain naturally alerts you to the danger by drawing your attention to the sabertooth. You're going to experience this as an initial feeling of fear. Virtually at the same time, your brain is going to initiate changes in your body. Before you saw the sabertooth, your brain had prioritized digestion of your recently consumed lunch and increased the blood flow to your stomach, but as soon as your brain registered the saber-toothed tiger, it shifted the blood flow away from your stomach and toward your major muscle groups (your arms and legs). This redirection of blood flow, together with an increase in your heart rate and respiration, prepares you to run away if you can and fight if you can't. Your brain achieves this sudden change by releasing a wash of chemicals, including adrenaline, into your bloodstream. These chemicals tell your body where to direct blood as well as speeding up your heart rate and your breathing.

Once your body has responded to the adrenaline (and other chemicals), it sends a message back to your brain saying, "I'm ready for action." This message is going to feel like "butterflies in the stomach" and perhaps shaking in your arms and legs due to the redirection of blood flow. You're also going to notice your pulse racing and the shift in your breathing, and you may even begin to feel light-headed as the additional oxygen is pumped into your brain. These are "somatic" emotions—emotions that you feel inside your body.

As these physical sensations reach your brain, your prefrontal cortex (executive brain) labels them as "fear." So you have two mental experiences of fear—the initial fear when you first see the sabertooth and a secondary feeling of fear based upon the physical changes in your body.

Some people notice the chemical wash being released that sends a message to the conscious mind, "I am beginning to feel afraid." They know they are beginning to feel afraid, even if they aren't necessarily experiencing the fear in their body just yet.

Other people pay more attention to the messages being sent back from their body, their heart, their stomach, and their arms and legs. These are the people who don't know that they are afraid—they simply feel the fear.

The same is true with positive emotions such as confidence, excitement, and joy. Some people know they are confident, and some people feel confident.

Our emotional system is a throwback to our days as simpler creatures when we did not have the ability to logically reason about what was going on around us. We have an immediate emotional response as a survival mechanism. So we can immediately feel fear, for example, when we first see the saber-toothed tiger without needing to take the time to "think" about it. By the time we have consciously thought about the sabertooth, it will have eaten us for lunch unless we are able to take action unconsciously.

Now, of course there are not very many saber-toothed tigers around in the modern world. We're more likely to feel fear when faced with an angry boss, client, or spouse. Fortunately, you do have the ability to override your immediate emotional response if you want to. Unfortunately, many people are neither aware that they have this control nor know how to exercise it. People very often feel as if they are at the mercy of their emotional responses, and on one level this is true. If you see a saber-toothed tiger, that information is routed to your amygdala, which responds by sending a message to your thalamus to generate adrenaline and other fear chemicals long before your rational mind has had the chance to realize that saber-toothed tigers are extinct and that what you actually saw was a shadow. That's the bad news. The good news is that there is something called the 90-second rule.

The 90-Second Rule

There is a little-known and very surprising fact about emotional states. And it's this: most emotional states are designed to last around 90 seconds, and 90 seconds only. It's as if nature decided that if you hadn't escaped from the saber-toothed tiger within 90 seconds, you were probably dinner anyway. So nature designed your emotions to give you the maximum amount of effect in a short space of time.

Now, I know you are thinking, "How can that be? I can feel good, or bad, for hours and days at a time." This is perfectly true. We all have had the experience of feeling something for a lot longer than a minute and a half. Ninety seconds is barely enough time to consciously recognize any kind of emotion or feeling, regardless of whether you tend to be someone who recognizes it and labels the emotion first or someone who feels it in the body first.

However, in order for any emotion to last longer than 90 seconds, the reality is that you are doing something inside your mind to maintain that emotional state. Think about it—if you feel bad for a long time, you are probably turning over some situation in your mind, making negative pictures inside your head, and saying bad things to yourself. You may be doing this consciously or unconsciously. Whichever way, it is happening! It is these thoughts that maintain the negative emotional feelings. In HNLP, we call this "throwing logs on the fire."

If you think of an emotional state as a bell curve, there is a beginning point, then the emotion will peak, and then it will begin to diminish. This process takes about 90 seconds. However, what tends to happen is that as the emotion begins to peak, we start to "throw logs on the fire," so to speak, by making pictures inside our mind, saying things to ourselves, and generally ruminating on the situation. This fuels the fire and maintains, or even increases, the emotion instead of allowing it to naturally diminish. Left to themselves, these feelings would begin to die away after 90 seconds or so.

Once you understand this 90-second rule, it is very easy to

change your state—you simply have to stop thinking about whatever it was that caused the negative emotion and wait for 90 seconds.

The opposite is also true: if you want to feel good for an extended period, continue to think great thoughts, make great pictures and movies in your head, and tell yourself great things. Of course, sometimes that is easier said than done!

Our Sensory System

The body is also impacted by the way we pay sensory attention to the world around us.

Before talking about this further, we want to point out that your senses do not give you an accurate view of the world around you. In fact, everything you see and hear and feel is created inside your own mind. Actually, this is not entirely true—most of the processing that your senses perform is carried out outside of your brain. For example, your eyes have ten times as many light-sensitive cells as neurons that go from your eyes to the visual cortex within your brain. So for every thousand light-sensitive cells in your eyes, there are only one hundred neurons that go from your eyes to your visual cortex. What this means is that ninety percent of the information being recorded by your eyes is not even sent to your brain. The reason for this is that your eyes are taking those thousand bits of information, processing that information within the eyes themselves, and only sending the results of that processed information to the visual cortex for further processing. In this sense, ninety percent of your visual processing actually takes place within your eyes.

A similar process has been shown to take place within the touch receptors of your skin. Much of the processing about touch, such as temperature, pressure, and texture, is carried out in your fingertips rather than in your brain.

Even when the sensory information reaches your brain, it is subject to much more processing before "you" see or hear or feel the world around you. You may, for example, have heard of the blind spot. The blind spot is the area of your retina where the optic nerve leaves your eye and makes its way back to your visual cortex. Because of this, the blind spot contains no light-sensitive cells—it is literally blind.

You can experience your blind spot by taking a piece of paper and drawing a small cross in the middle and a small circle about an inch to the right of the cross. Now cover your left eye, hold the paper in front of your face at about arm's length, and keep focusing your right eye on the cross as you slowly move the piece of paper toward you. At some point, you will find that the spot disappears; this is where the light from the spot is falling directly on your blind spot. The question is: "When the spot disappears, what do you see instead?" The answer is: "I see white" (or whatever color the paper is). Even though your blind spot is not recording any visual information, your brain makes the assumption that the area of the real world corresponding to your blind spot is the same color as the background around it. So if your eye sees a white piece of paper, it assumes that the area corresponding to the blind spot is also white, and it literally "fills in the gap."

This tendency of your eye to "fill in the gap" doesn't just apply to your blind spot. For example, if you hold your hand out at arm's length and look at your thumbnail, what do you see? It might not be what you think you see. In fact, only a very small part of your eye, called the fovea, actually sees things in detail. The only part of what you are looking at that is clear is probably the half-moon at the base of your thumbnail. Everything else—the rest of your nail, your thumb, your hand, and everything else in the room—is actually blurred, and it becomes progressively more blurred the farther away from your thumbnail it is. You experience what you see as being clearer than it really is because your brain fools you into thinking that the periphery of your eye (everything outside the fovea) sees clearly, when in reality it does not.

Because your eye is split into the fovea, which sees detail, and the periphery, which offers only a blurred sense of what might be there, your brain processes visual information in different ways. It pays active attention to what's in the fovea (for example, you are using your foveae to read this book) and more passive attention to what's in the periphery.

Your peripheral vision is in fact much better than the fovea at two important visual skills: seeing movement and seeing in the dark. While you are reading this book, your peripheral vision is constantly on the lookout for movements that may indicate something dangerous in your environment. For example, you may be reading this book in the park, and some inconsiderate teenager may have thrown a Frisbee at your head. As your peripheral vision sees the movements of the Frisbee, it alerts you to duck your head (hopefully in time to avoid being hit).

Your foveal vision and peripheral vision are actually processed by different parts of your brain, with your left brain being particularly interested in your foveal vision and your right brain being more interested in your peripheral vision.

Of course, this isn't how you actually experience the world. You experience the world as seamless, with vision, hearing, touch, taste, and smell all fully integrated. For example, have you ever reached the bottom of a flight of stairs only to realize you have miscalculated and found that there is one more step than you were expecting, leading you to almost fall? Or maybe one less step than you were expecting, resulting in a physical jarring when your foot hit the ground? This is because your eye told your body what to expect, and since your eye was fooled, your body was as well.

So not only do your senses and your brain (thoughts) act as one seamless system, but your senses and your physical body are also linked. Your senses are doing these sorts of sensory gymnastics all the time to fool you into thinking that you are experiencing the world "as it is" when in fact you are not. This leads to some interesting opportunities to utilize the quirks in your senses within the BEAT. For example, it has been found that going into peripheral vision tends to take your body into a "parasympathetic state" characterized by lower stress levels and more relaxation.

Your Thoughts

We have talked about your physical body, your emotions, and your senses. We can now ask the question: "What are your thoughts?"

On one level, your thoughts are any activity, any firing of neurons, that takes place inside your brain. However, much of this sort of neural activity is not something that you pay attention to, it is described by neuroscientists as, "transparent," meaning invisible to your conscious mind.

The kinds of thoughts that you can pay attention to are those that manifest as internal sensory experiences. For example, you might speak to yourself or hear your favorite song playing inside your head, you might see a picture or a movie in your mind, or you might imagine what it feels like to stroke your favorite pet or smell your grandmother's freshly baked bread or taste her chocolate chip cookies.

These internal sensory experiences join together in what is called "working memory." Your working memory consists of three aspects:

- a three-second movie clip
- a sound track to accompany the movie
- a title of the movie

Movies, along with their sound tracks and titles, are running constantly, and we are usually unaware of this happening. Now, of the three aspects, the title is probably the most important and has the most impact on our reactions (either conscious or unconscious). I once had a client who came for some personal change work. When we checked in on what movies he was running about his ideal outcome, he had wonderful images of success, a fantastic house, a sexy sports car, an expensive watch, a beautiful girlfriend—all the trappings of success! His sound track was a choir of angels. When I asked him what the title of this movie was, he replied, "I'll never have this." This title was limiting his ability to achieve the success in life that he desired. Here is another example. A colleague of mine tells of a client who had horrible images of a past event on her inner movie screen, coupled with an unpleasant sound track. However, the title of her movie was "I got through this, and it made me stronger."

The title we have assigned to these movies is all-important, as it creates the meaning of these internal experiences.

It is these three internal sensory experiences, the movie, the soundtrack and the title—our working memory—that we will be referring to when we use the word *thoughts*.

As we have discussed above, your thoughts impact, and are impacted by, both your physical body and your emotions. Obviously, the information you obtain from the outside world through your senses—your eyes, ears, nose, mouth, and skin—impact your thoughts. For example, you may see a supermarket delivery truck drive past and think, "That reminds me, I must buy some groceries on the way home."

Your thoughts also impact how you sense the world around you. Once again, you may believe that you simply see the world the way it is, but that is simply not true. The way you see the world is powerfully impacted by your thoughts. For example, think "blue," say "blue" to yourself, and see the color blue in your mind's eye. Now look around you. What do you notice? You probably found that all the blue objects around you jumped out of the background and were very noticeable. Try the same experiment thinking "'red" and you'll find that all the red objects seem to leap out at you.

This is not just about noticing a particular color in the world around you. The effect that your thoughts have on your sensory experience can be very profound and far-reaching. In one research study, subjects were asked whether or not they considered themselves lucky. They were then asked to search for certain words in a newspaper they were given. In the middle of the newspaper was a full-page ad that told them if they presented the page to the researcher, they would receive a sum of money. In general, the people who considered themselves lucky saw the ad and claimed their prize. Those who did not consider themselves lucky were more focused on finding the words they had been told to find and failed to see the ad. The subjects' belief about themselves as lucky or unlucky directly influenced the visual information they took in from the world around them.

The Neuroscience of Anchoring

Because the BEAT relies so heavily on anchoring, we will briefly discuss the neuroscience behind anchoring.

Neuroscience suggests that our brain likes to link related sensory experiences together. What does this mean? It simply means that when we see, or hear, or feel, or smell, or taste something, our brain looks around for other experiences that are present at the same time and links them together. For example, when Pavlov fed his dogs and rang a bell, the dogs began to associate the ringing of a bell with food. When this association had been made, Pavlov was able to make the dogs salivate simply by ringing the bell, without offering them food.

This association of two sensory experiences is a function of Hebb's Law, which states that "neurons that fire together, wire together." What this means is that when two neural circuits begin to fire at the same time, they become more permanently linked together, particularly with repetition and in the presence of a strong emotional response.

Let's take an example. A new neighbor moves in next door to you with his dog. As you pass his house, the dog runs out and savagely barks at you, startling you and making you back up. The next day, the same thing happens. On the third day, you are walking past your neighbor's house, and you see his dog. You automatically flinch, even though the dog does not bark at you this time. Your brain has begun to associate that particular dog with the feeling of being startled.

This is important for understanding how the concept of anchoring works. Anchoring takes an external stimulus—a "trigger" in the outside world—and attaches it to a feeling or a behavior. In NLP, we use this in a proactive way by attaching a positive feeling to a place (say, the podium, if you are giving a speech), a picture (perhaps your boss's face), a sound, or even a touch.

In the BEAT System, we will be using this association to link an external trigger, or rather a set of four external triggers, to four experiences: a physiological response, an emotional response, a sensory response, and a mental response (a thought).

Of course, this new pattern has to be conditioned in order for it to truly become an automatic response. If we think about Hebb's Law ("neurons that fire together, wire together"), the first time we run the pattern, we are simply firing these different neurons—just utilizing the first part of the "neurons that fire together" meme. In order to ensure that these neurons do "wire together," we have to run the pattern numerous times. This utilizes a process called long-term potentiation (LTP), which takes place through repeated cycles of the pattern. Therefore we have to run through the pattern numerous times with the client in order for the long-term potentiation to take place.

Once the BEAT System has been conditioned, it will be a simple matter for you to quickly and easily trigger that complete set of experiences, including your physiology, your emotions, your sensory experience, and your thoughts. This set of experiences, combined in the right way, will create your peak state.

Using the Mirror Neurons

As a final topic in this chapter, we will talk little bit about mirror neurons.

In a later chapter, we will talk about how you can find peak states for yourself by finding them in other people. Although this may sound odd, it is backed up by neuroscientific research. You see, within your brain you have specialized neurons called mirror neurons. The purpose of these neurons is to track the physical behaviors and emotions of the people around you and create a model of their experience within your own brain. While research is still being carried out on mirror neurons, it is believed that their purpose is to increase the level of rapport within a group by allowing you to feel the emotional states of others, and to allow you to learn physical skills faster by allowing you to physically "feel" what another person's actions feel like. We will be using the principles of mirror neurons in building peak states.

There is a certain amount of debate within the neuroscience world about the function of mirror neurons and even about the existence of mirror neurons within the human brain. This debate has been generated by the fact that mirror neurons can only be detected using electrical probes inserted into the brain, and therefore research on mirror neurons cannot be carried out on healthy humans. The debate has also been fueled by some overreach on the part of certain neuroscientists who have ascribed amazing results such as the birth of human civilization to mirror neurons in the absence of experimental data.

Having said this, it should be noted that nobody doubts that there is a mechanism within the human brain—whether mirror neurons or some other mechanism—that does what mirror neurons are reported to do. So whether these effects are actually caused by mirror neurons or by some other mechanism that is not currently known, we will use mirror neuron as the metaphor explaining these effects.

Section 2:

The Steps of the BEAT System

Chapter 3: Peak Performance States

What Is a Peak Performance State?

The purpose of the BEAT System is to create and install a peak state in you or your client. This begs the question: What is a peak performance state?

We could say that a peak performance state is a state in which somebody's performance on a specific task is as good as it can be. Clearly if the BEAT System can create this sort of peak performance state, the BEAT System is going to be an excellent tool for individuals who wish to excel as well as for coaches!

However, such a definition would not get us very far because we first need to know what a "state" is. Unless we know what a state is, we cannot know what a "peak performance state" is.

In NLP, a state is made up of several elements, including:

- The physiology of the body
- The emotions that are running through the body
- The state of mind, i.e., the thoughts that are being held in the brain
- The way in which the outside world is experienced through the senses

A state is "cybernetic," meaning that each of these elements of a state affects all the other elements of the state.

Try this experiment to experience how this interaction works:

First, stoop your shoulders, hang your head, make your breathing shallow, look down at your feet, and say: "I feel fantastic!!!" Notice how there is a mismatch between your body and what you are saying. Given this mismatch between what you say to yourself and your physiology, your emotions are likely to follow your body rather than your words.

Now try the opposite: pull your shoulders back, lift up your head, lift your chin, breathe deeply, and say: "I feel terrible!!!" You probably found it hard to feel terrible when your posture and physiology were resourceful!

So, your physiology is going to affect your emotional state. At the same time, your emotional state is going to affect your physiology. I'm sure you've seen a friend moping around with his or her shoulders and head slumped. You probably asked what was the matter because you knew from your friend's physiology that he or she was not in a good state.

Your thoughts are also going to affect your emotional state. Recall a recent time when something or somebody annoyed you, and you spent the day thinking about it. No doubt, your emotional state followed your thoughts; you thought about how annoying that event or person was and you felt annoyed.

In a similar way, your feeling of annoyance kept those negative thoughts running through your head. When you feel annoyed, your thoughts probably reflect that.

Your emotional state is also going to affect what you pay attention to in the outside world. If you're feeling down, you're likely to pay attention to negative aspects of the world around you. But when you're feeling joyful, you're more likely to pay attention to the happy things around you, and we say that you are looking at the world through "rose-colored glasses."

How you pay attention to the world around you will also impact how you feel, meaning that if you pay attention to joyful things around you, you are more likely to feel joyful. Once again, each part of the puzzle impacts each other part.

So all these elements of a state interact with the other elements of the state. The problem we often face, and the reason we're not usually in a peak state, is that each of these elements will also interfere with the others if they're not aligned. So you may be putting on the eighteenth green, but if your thoughts are still imagining the difficult meeting you had with your boss this morning or what you need to buy at the grocery store on the way home, you'll likely miss the putt. Or your eyes and brain are focused on your computer screen as you write that report, but the stiffness in your shoulders and your feeling of boredom make it hard to concentrate.

The whole purpose of the BEAT System is to bring all the elements of your state into alignment and make them all positive. When each element of the state is aligned with all the others, they become self-supporting; having a positive physiology will tend to make you feel more positive, which in turn will lead you to pay attention to positive things in the world around you, which will lead you to have positive thoughts, which in turn will tend to make your physiology more positive, and so on. A virtuous cycle is created.

Unlike some techniques that ask you to simply "think happy thoughts" regardless of your physiology, emotional state, or sensory perceptions, the BEAT System aligns your physiology, emotions, awareness, and thoughts to help you move in the direction of your goals and dreams.

Recognizing Peak States

Before we can enter a peak state at will, we need to be able to recognize what a peak state is. A good first step in recognizing peak states is to recognize when you see them in other people.

There are obvious places to look to see peak states, such as athletes who are performing at their best. The next time you watch a sporting event, take a look at a few of the best players on the field. Notice their physiology, their breathing, how they move, how they carry themselves, and their awareness of the space around them. Are they relaxed or tense, or somewhere in between? Notice the expression on their faces—do they seem happy or sad, or some other emotional state? Are they focused or defocused? Where is their sensory awareness, particularly what they are focusing on with their eyes?

You can also begin to pay attention to other people who are outstanding in their field. Perhaps you know individuals in your company who excel at what they do. When you see them doing what they do well, begin to pay closer attention to them. Again, notice how they stand, their physiology, how they move, how they carry themselves, how they breathe, their facial expression, and their attention. Notice their emotional state—are they happy or sad or determined, or some other emotional state?

You can also pay attention to the people around you in your everyday life, perhaps the people who serve you in a cafe or restaurant. Which of them appear to be in a peak state? Pay attention to your friends and relatives. Which of them appear to be in a peak state, and how do you know? What is it you're seeing that lets you know that they're in a peak state?

When you have begun to pay attention to people who are in a peak state, you can even begin to model them. Try standing the same way they stand. Try walking the same way they walk. Try adopting their facial expression. Hold your head the way they hold theirs. Match the way they breathe. Notice how you feel when you do.

Finding Internal Experiences of Peak States

The other place to find examples of peak states is inside you. You will need a piece of paper and something to write with for this exercise.

Peak State Exercise

Think back to a time in your life when you performed at your very best.

Recall that time and notice where you are—perhaps you're on the sports field or maybe at work. Go back to that time and notice the details of where you are. Who else is there? What is your physiology like? How are you feeling? What are you seeing? What are you hearing? What else are you paying attention to?

Now go back to a different time when you were in a peak state. Where are you this time? What is your physiology like? How are you feeling? What are you seeing? What are you hearing? What else are you paying attention to? Notice which parts of this experience are the same as, or different from, the previous one.

Record these impressions for each event:

- Where I am:
- Who else is there:
- My physiology (describe):
- How I'm feeling:
- What I'm seeing:
- What I'm hearing:
- What else I'm paying attention to:
- What I'm thinking:
- Which things are the same or similar for the two experiences:
- Which things are different for the two experiences:

As you begin to go back to more and more of those times when you had peak experiences and pay attention to them as if they were happening right now, you will begin to build a "database" of the elements that are part of a peak experience for you as an individual. This database will be extremely useful later on.

Achieving Success Through Peak States

You want the ability to enter into a peak state in order to achieve peak performance. And you want peak performance in order to achieve success. But what is success? And how will you know when you have achieved it?

In order to define success, you need to set appropriate goals and outcomes that are aligned with what is really important to you and who you really want to be as a person.

We will discuss this more in a later section of the book, but let's take a moment to consider what "success" might actually mean.

Feeling Great

One way of measuring success is to ask yourself these questions: "How am I feeling? How will I be feeling when I am successful?" You could say that if you spend your life feeling good, then you are successful. Indeed, many schools of philosophy take this very approach.

Flipping this around, if you spend your life feeling miserable, arguably you are not inwardly successful even if you are wealthy, famous, or have some other "badge" that tells the outside world you are successful. Many outwardly successful people in the modern world suffer from this type of lack of "inner success."

But enjoying life is not simply about feeling good—it is also about doing the things you value. According to this definition, success is ultimately about doing things that are important to you. You will be able to identify what things are important for you to do when you get in touch with your values. And when you get in touch with your values, you will better understand who you are, and who you want to be, as a person. Once you understand your values and who you wish to be as a person, you will find it easier to align your goals and behaviors with those values and that identity.

And if you discover that your purpose for being on Planet Earth is to feel good, then feeling good is what makes you successful. Therefore, being a master of your own deep emotions will make it much more likely that you will be a success.

In the next chapter, we will consider the NLP technique of anchoring. Anchoring will allow you to "capture" the peak states you have identified so that you can reexperience them at will.

Chapter 4: The BEAT and Anchoring

As we mentioned above, the BEAT System is an anchoring pattern. It involves two main types of anchors: spatial anchors and kinesthetic anchors. We will briefly mention other anchors that can also be brought into the pattern, such as visual and auditory.

What Are Spatial Anchors?

Spatial anchors are places, buildings, or simply spots on the floor or spaces in a room that evoke, or are "anchored to," certain feelings.

Spatial anchors are common in everyday life. If you see an Olympic athlete stepping onto the top step of the podium at the medal ceremony, you will see him or her immediately enter into a very powerful positive "victory" state. The podium represents a powerful spatial anchor for the athlete.

A powerful spatial anchor for a speaker is the speaker's podium. If you are a good speaker and you enjoy speaking, you probably feel really good when you step up to the podium to speak. However, if you have performance anxiety or stage fright, or simply do not enjoy speaking in public, you will probably feel nervous when you step up to the podium. Either way, the podium is a powerful spatial anchor that generates a powerful state.

There will be many other spatial anchors around you. For example, your sofa may be a spatial anchor for relaxation, your desk may be a spatial anchor for focus (or boredom!), the kitchen a spatial anchor for experimentation, or your fridge a powerful spatial anchor for snacking!

Your unconscious mind automatically associates certain spaces with certain activities. For example, the basketball court is a spatial anchor for playing basketball and might be a spatial anchor for a peak performance state if you happen to be great at playing hoops. Based on your location, your unconscious mind assumes that you will be engaging in an activity related to that place and provides you the state that it thinks will be most conducive to that activity.

Unfortunately, the unconscious mind does not necessarily choose the best state for you to be in, in that context—it simply chooses the state that has allowed you to succeed in the past, and for your unconscious mind, "success" is primarily measured by survival. Your unconscious mind is primarily focused on your survival, rather than on what you might consciously consider to be "success," because for the unconscious mind survival *is* success. Therefore, if you suffer from performance anxiety but "make it through" giving that speech or presentation, your unconscious mind might believe that becoming nervous is the correct and most useful state to experience. After all, that was the state you were in, and therefore that particular state helped you survive!

Spatial Anchors in the BEAT System

We will be using four locations on the floor as our spatial anchors in the BEAT System. These will be lined up in a straight line, 1-2-3-4 (actually, we will label them B-E-A-T). Setting kinesthetic anchors in this way will allow you to more easily use the BEAT System when coaching yourself.

Kinesthetic Anchors in the BEAT System

The other type of anchor that we will be using in the BEAT System is a kinesthetic anchor. A kinesthetic anchor is a touch that we apply to ourselves, or to our client, to go into a certain state. For example, a kinesthetic anchor in coaching may be a touch on someone's shoulder, or in self-coaching it may be squeezing the tip of your own thumb and the tip of your finger together.

In many ways, spatial anchors are easier to use; however, we will ask you to use both kinesthetic and spatial anchors because we want you to be able to use the BEAT System wherever you are and whenever you need it. If we only used spatial anchors, you would only be able to do the BEAT System in the place in which you set those anchors up! By using kinesthetic anchors, you will be able to take the BEAT System around with you and use it whenever you want. It will literally be "at your fingertips."

So we use both spatial and kinesthetic anchors at the same time. Spatial anchors make the pattern very easy to install, and kinesthetic anchors make the pattern very easy to take around with you.

The BEAT System breaks down your peak performance state into four pieces or elements:

- Body and breathing (physiology)
- Emotions
- Awareness of the outside world (senses)
- Thoughts

We will use four spatial anchors and four kinesthetic anchors to anchor these four elements of your peak performance state—one spatial anchor and one kinesthetic anchor for each of the four pieces of the state.

The spatial anchors will be laid out in a line in front of you (or your client), perhaps a foot apart, so that you can step easily from the first to the second to the third to the fourth.

The kinesthetic anchors that we use will be to squeeze the thumb of the right hand against each of the fingers of the right hand in turn, starting with the index finger and ending with the pinky.

These spatial anchors and kinesthetic anchors will be labeled B-E-A-T. If you wish, you can think of all this as providing auditory anchors (the sounds of the letters) and visual anchors (imagining the letters in your mind) in addition to the spatial and kinesthetic anchors.

Let's take a look at how these anchors will be used in practice during the basic BEAT:

Step one of the system will be to focus on the body and breathing, i.e., the physiology.

You (or your client) will stand one step away from the first spatial anchor. You will imagine seeing your ideal self standing on that first spatial anchor. You will see the posture and breathing, the facial expression, the look in the eyes, and the other physiological aspects of your ideal self.

When you can see your ideal self clearly, you will step

forward onto that first spatial anchor, stepping into your ideal self, and you will feel what it feels like physically to be your own ideal self. As you feel that, you will squeeze together the thumb and forefinger of your right hand. We label this first kinesthetic anchor "B" for body and breathing. Don't worry—we will go through each step in much more detail in later chapters.

The second spatial anchor will contain your emotional self. You will step forward onto the second spot in the ground and check in with your emotional state. If you are feeling good, you will fire the second kinesthetic anchor by squeezing the thumb and middle finger of your right hand together. We label this second kinesthetic anchor "E" for emotions. We will teach you a simple and powerful technique later on, in Chapter 6, that you can use if you step onto this second spot and do not feel so good.

When you are on the second spatial anchor, with a positive physiology and a positive emotional state, you are ready to move on to the third spatial anchor.

The third spatial anchor will be where you will check in with your sensory experience of the world around you— how you are paying attention to the world around you and your awareness. In a later chapter, we will teach you several different states of awareness and how to enter them.

As you begin to be aware of the world around you in a new way, you will fire the third kinesthetic anchor by squeezing together the thumb and ring finger of the right hand. This kinesthetic anchor is labeled "A" for awareness.

As you stand on the third spatial anchor, with a positive physiology, a positive emotional state, and resourcefully aware of the world around you, you are ready to step forward onto the fourth spot, the fourth spatial anchor, where you will check in with your thoughts.

As you step onto the fourth spatial anchor, you will begin to think the appropriate thoughts in the appropriate way. There are many ways to think and many things to think about. We will talk a lot more about how to think and what to think about in a later chapter.

As you begin to think positive thoughts, in an appropriate way, you will fire the fourth kinesthetic anchor by squeezing together the thumb and pinky finger of the right hand. This kinesthetic anchor is labeled "T" for thoughts.

Demonstration:

We will offer a quick demonstration to show how the above process works.

Coach: What would you like to work through today?

Client: I have to give a presentation next week, and I would like to feel a lot more confident about it.

Coach: Great, where is the presentation?

Client: It's in the office. I'll be giving it in the boardroom.

Coach: Great, and what do you want to achieve in the presentation?

Client: I want to convince them to go ahead with my project.

Coach: And when you get to the end of the presentation, how will you know if you have achieved that? What will you see that will let you know that they are in favor of your project? I know that at some stage they will tell you, but what will you see right there and then that will let you know your presentation has been a success?

Client: I guess I would see them smiling and nodding.

Coach: Okay, great. Today we are going to do a system called the BEAT System. This system is going to provide you with a great sense of confidence and much, much more than that. Are you ready to try it?

Client: Sure!

Coach: Okay, so stand there. Take a look at the floor in front of you and pick out four spots. These will be the stepping-stones to your success. Make them so that you can easily step from one to the other, perhaps around there, there, there, and there [pointing to the ground], but you can pick whichever spots feel good now to you.

Client: Okay, that sounds good.

Coach: Now I would like you to take your right hand—can you spell BEAT? B-E-A-T? That's right, now squeeze your thumb against each of your fingers in turn as you spell BEAT, B-E-A-T. As you step forward, you will be using each of those anchors, "B" for that first stepping-stone, "E" for that second stepping-stone, "A" for that third stepping-stone, and "T" for that final stepping-stone.

Client: Okay, got it.

Coach: Great, so as you take a look at that first stepping-stone, I would like you to imagine that you could see yourself standing there. As you see yourself standing there, you see your ideal self, the "you" who will be able to give a great presentation, feeling totally confident, so that at the end they will be smiling and nodding. Do you see that?

Client begins to straighten his posture, and his breath deepens.

Client: Yes, I can see that!

Coach: Great, what exactly do you see?

Client: I see myself there, I'm sort of... I'm leaning forward a little. I have a look of intensity...

Coach: That's right! You're leaning forward a little, and you have a look of intensity. Now when you're ready, step forward into that "you"—really feel what it feels like to have that sense of intensity, to know that you can do it, to be your best!

[Client steps forward, and his posture improves even more. A smile comes to his face.]

Coach: How does that feel?

Client: That feels great!

Coach: Great! And as you're feeling that now, squeeze your thumb and forefinger together. That's "B" for body and breathing. Feel how great that feels. Now, as you're feeling great, I'd like you to step forward onto the second stepping-stone.

[Client steps forward.]

Coach: Now I'd like you to check inside and notice how good you're feeling.

Client: I feel great. I really feel confident.

Coach: Where do you feel that?

Client: In my chest.

Coach: Great! Now I would like you to squeeze your thumb and middle finger together, that's "E" for emotions... Do you remember learning the "stop the world" state?

Client: Yes, that's the peripheral vision, right?

Coach: Right... Okay, when you step forward onto the third stepping-stone, you're going to go into the "stop the world" state. Got it?

Client: Yes, I got it.

[Client steps forward onto the third stepping-stone. The focus of the client's eyes changes.]

Coach: That's right! Now squeeze your thumb and ring finger together. That's "A" for awareness. And now as you step forward onto the fourth and final stepping-stone, I want you to make a picture in your mind of your audience during the presentation smiling and nodding as you talk about your project. Step forward now.

[Client steps forward onto the fourth stepping-stone.]

Coach: What's happening now?

Client: Wow. I feel great.

Coach: Okay, let's do that again. Come back to the start, and see your ideal self on the first stepping-stone. Step into that and feel how good it feels to stand in that way, to breathe in that way. As you do, squeeze your thumb and forefinger together. "B." Now step forward onto the second stepping-stone. How does that feel?

Client: That feels awesome!

Coach: That's right, it does feel awesome! And now squeeze your thumb and middle finger together. That's "E" for emotions. Now step forward onto the third stepping-stone, Stop the world! Squeeze that thumb and ring finger together. "A." And now step forward on the fourth stepping-stone, and see the audience smiling and nodding as you talk about your proposal.

[The system is repeated several more times.]

Coach: Now I would like you to imagine being in the boardroom next week. It's time for you to step up and give your presentation. As you step forward, you feel yourself stepping over those stepping-stones. As you do, you begin to fire off those anchors, B-E-A-T. Try it now.

Client closes his eyes and runs through the instructions. He fires the anchors with his right hand.

Coach: How's that?

Client: That felt great!

Key Points

Here are the key points from this introductory section.

A peak state is what makes the difference between success and failure. A peak state allows you to achieve your goals, be a success, and be happy.

Any state is made up of several elements. These include your physiology—how you are using your body. But we're not only concerned with how you use your body to interact with the world around you; we're also concerned with how you are using your body internally, meaning your emotional state inside your body. Your peak state also involves how you look at the world around you, how you use your awareness of the world around you. And it also involves your thoughts—not just what you think about but also how you think about it.

Sometimes these elements act against each other; for example, perhaps you're thinking about how to succeed but are feeling nervous. Or perhaps you're focused on what you want when you're standing in an un-resourceful posture. The BEAT System is designed to align each element of your state so they reinforce each other.

States can be "anchored" using spatial or kinesthetic anchors, so they can be available to you whenever you wish.

Each element of your peak state can be anchored separately. When these anchors are fired sequentially (called "chaining anchors" in NLP), they supercharge your peak state.

In the chapters that follow, we're going to go into more depth on each element of the peak state as well as how to put the whole thing together.

Of course, a peak state is useless unless you actually take action. Taking action allows you to move forward toward your goals. Sometimes your actions may not go the way you want, which can take you out of your peak state. You need to have sufficient control over your state to be able to step back into your peak state when you need to. We'll talk more about how to take the appropriate action in later chapters.

Chapter 5: Body and Breath-The Physiology of Excellence

Your grandma was right when she told you to sit up straight and not to slouch. After all, as we discussed in Chapter 3, there is a direct link between the body and the mind—the so-called mind-body connection.

Our modern lifestyle, spending hours sitting in front of a computer, does nothing for our postures, or at least nothing good! The rise of the chiropractic profession over the last thirty years or so speaks to how out of touch we have become with the most basic aspects of our own posture. Take a look around the next time you are in a public place, and you'll see why: people standing with all their weight on one leg or the other, but not evenly distributed between the two; people with their spines curved and their heads hanging as they look down at the smartphone held in front of their stomach; people taking shallow breaths from their upper chest. These habitual patterns influence how we feel in the moment and may cause serious medical problems later in life.

It's easy to see the connection that leads from your body to your mind; all you have to do to radically change your thoughts is to stub your toe! And it's easy to see the connection that leads from your body to your feelings; all you have to do to change how you feel is to get a nice massage!

But how can you consciously change your physiology, right now, to change your thoughts and your emotions? Let's try a quick exercise to find out.

Exercise

Take a moment now to stand up. First, check in with how you're feeling, your emotional state. And now check in with your thoughts. In particular, how are you feeling about yourself, the world, and your place in it?

Shake out any tension you may feel—literally shake your hands, your arms, and your shoulders. Gently rotate your head. Take a deep relaxing breath in and slowly breathe out.

Now imagine that there is a silver thread connecting the top of your head to the sky so that your spine is hanging down from that thread. Notice how this tends to lengthen and loosen your spine. Simply by visualizing this thread, you'll begin to stand straighter. Imagine that the thread is pulling upward, stretching and lengthening your spine even farther.

Now begin breathing from deep in your stomach, from a place in the center of your body three inches below your belly button. This is said to be the center of your internal energy as well as your center of gravity. Put your attention on this point and, using your diaphragm, allow your stomach to move out when you breathe in, and in when you breathe out, so your breathing becomes deeper. Begin to count your breaths in and out, allowing your out-breath to be twice as long as your in-breath. For example, you may breathe in to a count of three and out to a count of six.

Notice your feet on the floor. Imagine that they are rooted, with roots flowing down into the earth. Literally feel energy flowing through your feet and into the floor as if it's filling a reservoir of energy beneath you. Feel the gravity holding you to the planet. Shift your weight slightly forward and backward, from side to side, and notice how your balance shifts. As you do so, keep your attention on your center of gravity.

Now notice how you feel—your emotional state. And notice your thoughts—what you're thinking about yourself, the world, and your place in it. Notice how your feelings and thoughts have changed from before you started the exercise.

The important thing about this exercise is to begin to simply pay attention to your own physiology. When you're able to pay attention to your own physiology, you will know when you are firmly rooted, when you're breathing deeply using your diaphragm, when your head is floating and your spine is elongated.

You will also know if your spine is not aligned, for example, if it stoops over or twists to the left or the right. And you will recognize if you are unbalanced rather than rooted and when your physical center shifts from your center of gravity. And you will notice when you are not breathing deeply using your diaphragm.

It's extremely worthwhile to spend the time to become more self-aware in relation to your physiology. By becoming more self-aware, you can make conscious adjustments and spend more of your day in a more ideal physical alignment:

- Alignment of your spine
- Alignment of your "center" with your center of gravity
- Alignment of your weight over your feet
- Alignment of your breathing

Your Physiology Is Controlled by Your Thoughts

Not only does your physiology influence your thoughts, but the opposite is also true.

Research has shown that the mind controls every aspect of the body, and not merely through movement and conscious breathing. Your mind also controls your unconscious breathing and your heartbeat as well as digestion, cell regeneration, and a multitude of other physical processes.

What and how you think causes your body to respond according to your thoughts. When you read emotional words, you begin to become emotional, and when you read action words such as "I am running," your body begins to react as if it were about to run.

When you make images in your mind of you being a certain way—let's say standing in a certain way—your body automatically begins to adopt that physiology. That's why imagining a thread suspending the top of your head from the sky, elongating your spine upward, is not just a metaphor—it actually *causes* your spine to lengthen. And that's why putting your attention on your center of gravity *causes* your balance to improve. And that's why imagining energy flowing from you and into the floor *causes* you to feel more rooted.

A person's body also responds to thoughts that are in the form of words, or self-talk. If people tell themselves that they are feeling nervous, their physiology begins to reflect nervousness. And when their physiology reflects nervousness, they begin to feel nervous on an emotional level. And when they feel nervous on an emotional level, their body sends a signal back to their prefrontal cortex telling them that they're feeling nervous. And when they feel the signal from their body telling them that they are feeling nervous, they say to themselves, "I'm feeling nervous." It's a self-fulfilling prophecy, a negative spiral. That is how people talk themselves into negative states.

Fortunately, the opposite is also true. When you tell yourself that you are confident and you make an image of yourself being confident, your physiology begins to reflect that confidence. The more strongly you imagine that picture, the more physiologically confident you become. And the more your physiology reflects confidence, the more confident you feel. This can create a virtuous circle (or upward spiral) of confidence. We say "can" because if any one of these pieces is out of alignment, it changes everything and may recreate a negative spiral.

And that's why the BEAT System focuses on each of these pieces in turn. This is how the BEAT System is so effective at creating your ideal state. The BEAT directs positive energy into each element of your state: your physiology, your feelings or emotions, your awareness of the world around you, and your thoughts. Each of these goes on to influence all the others in a positive way. They build and support each other to create your peak state.

Now, an interesting aspect of this is that it also works when thinking about or imagining somebody else. In an earlier chapter, we discussed mirror neurons and the effect they have on you. When you see somebody standing confidently, for example, your mirror neurons begin to fire off, and a part of you begins to feel confident as well.

We will be using this phenomenon when we practice the BEAT System by imagining seeing someone you admire who exemplifies the peak state you are looking for. Seeing the person in that positive state will cause you to begin to move into the same positive state.

Let's take a moment to explore how this works using the following exercise.

Exercise: New Behavior Generator

The following exercise is taken from NLP and is called the New Behavior Generator. In Chapter 9, we will be combining this technique with the anchor for the "B" of the BEAT System to create one application of the BEAT, called the DTI BEAT. For now, just play along with this exercise.

Let's give this a quick practice run. I'd like you to think about somebody you admire and who has a quality you would like to have as well. For example, many of my male clients who come to see me because they are shy or have some social anxiety choose James Bond! Whoever you choose, make a picture of that person in your mind. Read through the rest of the instructions before you begin or have someone else lead you through the exercise.

Now stand up. Imagine this person is standing in front of you. Notice their posture, their physiology. Notice how they are breathing. Notice their facial expression and the position of their head. Notice how they stand, how their weight is balanced. Notice their eyes and where they are looking.

Make this picture big—life-sized and maybe even a little larger. Make it bright and colorful. You might also want to add a sound track. Perhaps you hear their voice, and maybe there is even music playing (the James Bond theme song, perhaps!).

When the picture is perfect, just the way you want it, you might want to add a title to it. The title of the picture is included in your working memory, after all. As we described in Chapter 2, the title of the movie that plays in your working memory creates the meaning of that internal experience for you. You might want to choose a title such as "It is awesome to have the confidence of James Bond!" (or whomever you have chosen). This title simply lets your unconscious mind know what to do with the picture.

Now take a step forward so you literally step inside the picture. As you do so, feel how good it feels to be able to adopt that physiology.

Now step out of the picture again. Take another look at the picture. Perhaps you want to make it bigger or brighter. Make any changes you want to make and when you are ready, step back inside them. Feel how good that feels. Step back out.

Now we're going to play a little game. Once more, see the model in front of you and make the picture big and bright. Step into it again and feel how good that feels. This time, as you step forward into the picture, don't step out—instead see a second picture of the person in front of you, this time even bigger and even brighter.

In a moment, you are going to step into that second picture, and when you do, those good feelings are going to double. See that second picture in front of you and step into it, feeling those good feelings double.

Now see a third picture of the person in front of you, this time even bigger and even brighter. When you step into that third picture, the feelings are going to double again! Step into it now and feel how amazing it feels.

Once again, see the picture in front of you even bigger and brighter, and—you guessed it—when you step into that picture, the feelings will double again! Step into it now and feel the feelings double. Feel how awesome that feels Now triple, or even quadruple those good feelings, and notice how amazing this feels!

Practice this until it becomes second nature, until you can step into a picture of somebody you admire, somebody who has qualities you want to emulate, and really begin to feel how you imagine it may feel. By repeating this process, you can multiply those good feelings manay times over.

When you can do this easily, you can add a kinesthetic anchor. All you have to do is to imagine the person standing in front of you once more. Make the picture big and bright, and step into them. As you do so, you will begin to feel those good feelings rise up, and as they do, simply squeeze the thumb and forefinger of your right hand together (this is the "B" anchor of the BEAT System).

Enjoy the good feelings for a few seconds, and then as these feelings begin to subside, step out of the image and allow your thumb and forefinger to separate.

Step back into the picture, feeling those great feelings and once more squeezing your thumb and forefinger together, "B." As the feeling subside, step out and release the anchor.

Repeat the sequence a few more times to condition the anchor.

Now try simply squeezing your thumb and forefinger together. You should feel those good feelings arise all by themselves!

Body Scanning

Body scanning is a process that allows you to internally check out your own physiology. To show you how to do this, here is a quick exercise.

Exercise: Body Scanning

Read all the instructions before you begin this exercise.

Stand up and either close or defocus your eyes so that you can move your attention inside. Become aware of your body. Begin at the top of your head and slowly move your attention down your body. As you do so, give particular attention to the following:

- Your orientation in space, and your balance
- The alignment of your head, spine, hips, and feet in relation to the ground
- The orientation of your hands and arms relative to your body
- The orientation of your feet relative to each other
- The feeling of your clothing and the air around you on your skin
- Any areas of tension within your muscles, tendons, and skeleton
- The feelings within your vital organs, especially your heart, lungs, and stomach, including your heartbeat
- Your rate and depth of breathing

When you're ready, open your eyes and come back into the room.

As a coach, it's a great skill to be able to look at your clients and scan the various elements of their physiology, such as their posture, breathing, gestures, eye movements, and so on. You can combine this information with their feelings, or how they report those feelings to you, to begin to build a picture of when they are in a positive or negative state, simply based upon your visual scan. This allows you to direct your change work more accurately.

Exercise: Body Scanning with Adjustment

Now repeat the above body scanning exercise, this time allowing your body to make changes and adjustments. So, for example:

- If you find you are unbalanced, or if your head, spine, hips, and feet are not in alignment, allow your spine to lengthen, your weight to move to your center of gravity, and your weight to sink a little into the ground until you're back in balance and alignment.
- If you find that your hands and arms, or your feet, are not even and symmetrical, allow them to come into symmetry.
- If you feel any tension in your muscles, tendons, or skeleton, allow that to dissolve.
- If you feel that your breathing is too rapid or too shallow, allow it to slow and deepen.

Repeat this exercise several times until it becomes second nature.

When you're able to do a body scan and make suitable adjustments, easily and naturally, you're ready for the next exercise. This exercise will set us up for another version of the BEAT, called the Ideal-Self BEAT. We will get to the Ideal-Self BEAT in Chapter 9, but for now we will consider the first step only.

First Step of the Ideal-Self BEAT

See an image in front of you of your ideal self. Make this picture bright, three-dimensional, and slightly bigger than life-size. Give this picture a title—perhaps something like

"My Ideal Self"—and an awesome sound track!

Notice how your ideal self stands, how he or she breathes, facial expression, gestures, and so on.

Now step forward into your ideal self, taking on the gestures, facial expression, breathing, and physiology of your ideal self. As you do so, do a body scan to ensure that your body is aligned, inside and out, with your ideal self. Allow any necessary adjustments to take place.

As usual, when your physiology becomes that of your ideal self, squeeze your thumb and index finger together, "B."

Now that we've considered the "B" of the BEAT System, let's move right ahead to the "E."

Chapter 6: Mastering Your Emotions

I don't know if you have ever taken time to consider emotions—what emotions are, what emotions do for us, and how we can master our emotions.

For many people, the word *emotion* is used to explain a mood, an "affect," a state, or a feeling. We all experience emotions, and yet we may not have taken the time to explore what they are and how they impact us.

Many people believe that they are at the mercy of their emotions—that these feelings come and go throughout the day, impacting us, changing our behaviors, and affecting our thought processes, all without our having any control over them. They may believe, "Emotions can't be controlled. I feel what I feel. I'm not responsible. I'm a victim. Someone else made me feel bad. I need someone else to make me feel good."

The interesting thing is that we have full control over our emotions, should we so choose. For some, that control is entirely unconscious, and we will be talking about how we unconsciously control our emotions a little later.

Through personal insights and through practice, people gain conscious control over their emotions. I remember a televised interview that the British travel writer Michael Palin had with the Dalai Lama. Palin was sharing his amusing experiences in Dharamsala, the village in India that acts as the Dalai Lama's home in exile. Suddenly Palin switched gears and asked the Dalai Lama about the state of Buddhism in Tibet, a subject one would expect would be very sensitive to the exiled leader of the Tibetan Buddhists, and indeed, the Dalai Lama's face flushed. But rather than expressing what might have been an emotionally charged opinion, the Dalai Lama simply sat still for a short time, his face returned to normal, and then he spoke, inviting Palin to travel to Tibet to find out for himself. This is a wonderful example of state control.

We will be talking about this technique for self-control a little later. Although, again, your grandmother may have taught you the same technique when you were a young child!

The Evolutionary Basis of Emotions

On an evolutionary basis, our emotions serve a very important purpose: they let us know what we should be doing, and they put our body and physiology in the perfect state to do it. The word *emotion* literally means "to move out." This reflects the fact that our emotions give us the energy to act in the world.

For example, think about "fight, flight or freeze." When our ancestors were confronted by a predator, they had to either freeze, run away if they could, or fight if they couldn't escape. They didn't have time to consciously think about it—they simply had to react. The freeze action may have given them a moment to unconsciously "decide" to remain frozen, to run away or to stay and fight. And when they had to run or fight for their lives, they had to put one hundred percent effort into that, or else they wouldn't have survived. And if they hadn't survived, you would never have been born. In order to survive, they had to release adrenaline and other chemicals into their body to supercharge their normal physical responses.

Alternatively, consider when two of your ancestors first met, gazed into each other's eyes, and fell in love. The emotion we call "love" bonded them together and allowed them to successfully raise children, one of whom was another of your ancestors!

Emotions Are a Reflection of Our Internal Experiences

Emotions can be thought of as a reflection of our internal experience (as are all our behaviors, such as our breathing, gestures, posture, and so on).

Before we create these internal experiences, we have experiences of the world around us. We take in information from around us via our five senses. We see things, hear things, physically touch things, are aware of our proprioception, smell things, and taste things. These experiences make up our life—the contexts in which we find ourselves, the people we interact with, and the things we do. Everything we experience, we experience through our senses.

This information is taken in using our external senses but then goes through internal processing. During this internal processing, we make meanings, we make value judgments, we compare and contrast things, and we measure them against our personal beliefs, past experiences (memories), and future dreams. We sort, label, and categorize this information unconsciously as part of this internal processing. We carry out this internal processing by making internal pictures, sounds, and dialogue to make sense of our external experiences.

Of course, this process happens largely on an unconscious level. We process tremendous amounts of information within fractions of a second. Depending upon the images, judgments, and connections, we create meaning, and this meaning causes our brain to release a mixture of different chemicals. This chemical cocktail washes through our brain and body, causing us to experience emotions and behave in certain ways.

Different chemicals will be released according to the meanings we place on different experiences. If we see a nice ripe strawberry, we might make the meaning "I want to eat you!" But if we see a saber-toothed tiger, we will more likely to make the meaning, "He wants to eat me!" The meaning we make from each experience is different, and so is our internal response.

So our brain will release certain chemicals when we are experiencing hunger or love, and a different combination of chemicals when we are experiencing fear or anger. This process happens so quickly that it is difficult for us to notice whether the chemicals are released due to our internal experiences or whether the external experience provokes the release of such chemicals. In fact, we tend to lose track of the internal processing that takes place between the external sensory experience and our brain and body releasing the chemical cocktail representing the emotional response to an experience.

So, emotions are caused by the meanings made by our

internal processing of all external sensory experiences. Our emotions are the last link in a chain of external and internal events, most of which are invisible to us. In HNLP, we say that the emotion is the "caboose of the train." If all you notice is your emotional response to situations, you are failing to see the engine and the carriages that have been rolling down the track ahead of it.

In order to regain control of our emotions, we have to become aware of this chain of events so that we can make changes at the appropriate link in the chain. Our unconscious mind is doing the best it can to select the right emotion for any situation, but it is constrained by millions of years of evolution that cause it to see any threat as being immediate. It is rather like taking a crack team of military commandos and putting them in charge of a kindergarten!

The good news is that your unconscious mind can be retrained to select emotions that will serve you better. All you have to do to begin this process is to learn the language of the unconscious mind. Remember the 90-second rule? That's the amount of time it takes your amygdala to send a message to the thalamus; the thalamus to release adrenaline and other emotion-creating chemicals into your bloodstream; your heart, lungs, stomach, muscles, and other internal organs to respond; and that response to fade away again as the chemicals dissipate in your bloodstream.

If you wait for those 90 seconds, you can literally choose a new emotional response, you can choose a new emotion. This is precisely what the Dalai Lama did in the interview with Michael Palin—he waited for the emotion to pass while keeping his mind still, avoiding "throwing logs on the fire." We will be talking about how to incorporate this 90-second rule within the BEAT System.

When you are in control of your emotional responses, we say that you are "at cause." This means that nothing and no one else "makes" you feel a certain way. You take responsibility for your own emotional state. How will your life be different when you have total control over your emotions?

Emotions Are Signals from the Body

Another way to think of emotions is that they are reflections from our body, both internally and externally. When the brain releases neurotransmitters and other chemicals into the body, they have specific physiological effects, such as speeding up or slowing down the heart rate and breathing, increasing or decreasing the rate of digestion of food, decreasing or increasing blood flow to the muscles and brain, or increasing blood flow to the skin when we blush at the sight of an attractive potential mate.

When internal organs and muscles are impacted in this way, they send a signal back to the brain to let the brain know that they are ready for action. It is the signals coming back from the body, such as butterflies in the stomach, that we interpret as bodily emotions.

In this sense, emotions are therefore signals—signals from the belly, from the chest, from the arms and legs, from the hands, from the face—to the brain. The purpose of these signals is to let the brain know that the body is ready for whatever actions are required, such as fight, flight, or freeze. The brain then interprets, and names, these emotions.

As we discussed in the previous chapter, aspects of your physiology that fall under your conscious control, such as your posture, breathing rate, and so on also have a direct effect on your emotions and state. Your brain doesn't distinguish between physiological responses that are not under your conscious control (such as your heartbeat) and those that are within your conscious control (such as your breathing). So by using your mind to consciously control your physiology, you control the signals your body sends back to your brain, which directly changes your emotions.

So while we've been saying that your external sensory experiences lead to your internal processing, and your internal processing creates meaning that leads to a release of chemicals as an emotional response, and this emotional response changes your physiology, it is not as simple as that. It really is a case of which comes first, the chicken or the egg. Each link in the chain affects every other link.

Naming Emotions

Another way to think of emotions is by using the labels we put on them. We've been talking about emotions such as fear or confidence, love, anxiety, and desire.

We learn from an early age the names of emotions. As a small child, your mother or other adults told you that you were feeling happy, sad, angry, and so on. You began to associate these words with the feelings you had at that time.

And yet emotions are entirely subjective. It's impossible to tell if your experiences of happiness and my experience of happiness are identical. If two people say they are experiencing happiness, how can we tell if their experiences are the same? The words we use to label emotions not only allow us to communicate with each other about how we are feeling, but they can also limit us to feeling only those emotions that we have words or labels for.

Dissociating and Associating into Emotions

In my work with clients, I have found that people broadly fall into two main categories when considering emotions. Firstly, there are those who intellectually recognize an emotion yet have a hard time connecting to it physically.

We say these people are more "dissociated" from their emotions. For these people, emotions may mainly represent the *labels* that they give to feelings—"I feel angry," "I feel happy," "I feel confident"—rather than the somatic feelings they actually have in the body. When I see clients who are more dissociated from their emotions, they may use words to tell me how they feel, but when I ask them *where* in their body they feel the emotion, they looked at me blankly, as if the question doesn't make sense.

And then there are those who are very aware of how their body is responding to their emotions. We say these people are more "associated" to their emotions. For these people, emotions represent the actual somatic feelings—the feelings in their body. I have some clients who can become totally overwhelmed by the physicality of their emotions. They feel them so strongly within the body that it's like an energy that makes them shake.

The concept of associating and dissociating from emotions is vital in NLP and HNLP coaching as well as in the BEAT System itself.

John Overdurf's Self-Coaching Pattern

Here we will show you a simple method to let go of negative emotions by stopping negative thoughts, and increasing positive emotions by focusing on positive thoughts.

The first, and in many ways the most important, skill for letting go of negative emotions is to be able to notice your emotional state in the first place. To do this, you must get in touch with how your body feels and what that feeling means.

Take a moment now to scan your body from head to foot and just notice what you notice. Notice any areas within your body that capture your attention.

Now I'd like you to think of a good memory, a really good memory. Imagine you are back in that time and place, seeing what you saw and hearing what you heard. As you do so, notice how your feelings change within your body; you probably begin to feel some of the positive emotion you felt in that past experience. As you feel that now, go inside and notice where in your body you feel it, perhaps in your chest or your shoulders. Just notice where it is.

As you notice where in your body the feeling is, notice the size and shape of the feeling. Is it more like a tennis ball, a softball, or a basketball? Perhaps it's round, square, or more like a tube. Just experience what the feeling is like. Notice if there is a movement or a vibration to the feeling. Perhaps there is a temperature. Perhaps there is even a color. Just notice what comes to mind when you put your attention on that feeling.

Now we will show you a great way to get rid of a negative feeling. This exercise is used in many forms of mindfulness and meditation, and relies upon the 90-second rule. In this form, it is based upon John Overdurf's self-coaching pattern.

Exercise

Please read the entire instructions through before you start so you will find it easy to allow the negative feelings to disperse.

This time, think of a memory that is slightly negative. Perhaps you are waiting in line in the post office, and it is taking a long time to get served—something minor like that. Imagine you are back in that time and place, seeing what you saw and hearing what you heard. Begin to notice that original frustration or whatever the negative feeling is.

Once again, notice where in your body you feel it, and notice the size, shape, and color of the feeling.

Once you notice the size, shape, and color of the feeling, use those attributes to label it. So rather than saying, "I am frustrated," instead say, "The feeling that I'm feeling is the size of a softball in the center of my chest, and it's red" or whatever the appropriate description is for you. Simply put your attention on the feeling as a physical sensation in your body and notice what happens.

If you do this, without thinking about the event or what it meant to you, without throwing logs on the fire, the emotion will begin to subside after 90 seconds or less. As the feeling subsides, the size or shape or location or color of the feeling will begin to change. Typically it becomes smaller, for example, although for some people it may get larger but less intense as it dissipates.

Keep your attention on the location, size, shape, and color of the feeling until it disappears or is entirely transformed into something else.

Once the feeling has gone, you have to decide what to replace it with. After all, you cannot go around feeling nothing (unless you are a zombie!). We find that the easiest way to pick an appropriate positive emotion is using the "self-coaching" developed by John Overdurf.

Simply ask yourself three questions. The first question is:

"Aside from this, what's everything else that I haven't been paying attention to until now?"

Give yourself a few moments to allow the answer to this question to arise. It is not a question designed for your conscious mind, so don't try and find the "right" answer.

Just allow whatever comes to mind. Then ask yourself the second question:

"And with all of that, what's important to me about being here, now?"

Allow your unconscious mind to find something that is really important to you, a value that you hold. When you identify a value, ask yourself the third question:

"How am I expressing that in my life right now? And when I am expressing that in my life, where am I feeling it in my body, now?"

So for example, if the answer to the second question is "freedom," the third question might be something like:

"How am I being free in my life right now?"

Although this sounds like a slightly strange process, what we are doing is allowing your unconscious mind to choose a resource, a value, that is truly important to you. We then begin to turn that into an emotion (in this case, a feeling in the body) by noticing where you feel that within your body. This replaces the old negative emotion with something much more useful.

Increasing and anchoring positive emotions

So what should you do if you go inside and find a positive emotion, or if you transform a negative emotion into a positive emotion using the Self-Coaching Pattern? Once you have identified the positive emotion or have transformed the negative emotion into a positive emotion using the 90-second rule, you might want to increase this positive feeling and keep it around for longer than 90 seconds!

To do this, all you have to do is to once more pay attention to where in your body the emotion is, along with its size, shape, and color, but this time intensify these. You can make the emotion bigger, make the color brighter if it has a color, and so on. This is another form of "throwing logs on the fire," but this time with a positive emotion.

So if you're feeling confidence, and that confidence feels like a red ball in your chest the size of a tennis ball, you might want to say to yourself, "I feel confidence in my chest, it's the size of a tennis ball, and it's growing bigger!" As you do so, imagine the ball increasing in size. Then you might say, "The ball is red and is getting brighter!" Once again, imagine the ball becoming brighter. Each time you do this, you're instructing your conscious mind to intensify feelings.

Once you're feeling that positive feeling inside yourself and you have intensified it, you're going to anchor it by squeezing the thumb and middle finger of your right hand together. This is the "E" anchor of the BEAT System.

So to recap, feel a positive emotion, make it bigger and brighter, add more movement, do whatever you need to do to "throw logs on the fire" and make that emotion stronger. When the emotion feels really strong, squeeze your thumb and middle finger together, "E."

Repeat this a few times to create a strong anchor.

Once you've done this, you can test it by squeezing your thumb and middle fingers together and noticing that emotion beginning to well up in your body.

Anchoring emotions in this way gives you a great tool to control your emotional state.

Conclusion

The more you mindfully pay attention to your emotions, locating them within your body and noticing their qualities (size, shape, movements, and color), and experience the choice of replacing negative emotions with positive ones, the easier it will become to master your own emotions.

Chapter 7: Awareness of Your Senses

As we've mentioned several times in this book, the only way to take in information from the world around you is through your external senses—your senses of sight, hearing, touch, and so on. And the only way you can imagine the world around you is using your internal senses.

Each external sense has a corresponding internal sense. So, for example, you can see something in front of you, or you can imagine seeing the same thing in front of you. In fact, your external senses and internal senses use the same parts of your brain to create pictures.

Your sensory experiences, external and internal, form an important part of your experience in the moment. Using your senses to their best effect is part of your peak experience. We will discuss how to do this in detail below.

The Five Senses

We have five senses that allow us to take in information from the outside world: sight, hearing, taste, smell, and feeling.

In fact, we have a lot more than five senses, but we traditionally simplify things by grouping them together, particularly under the heading of feeling. This really does a disservice to your ability to sense because we tend to forget about senses such as proprioception—your ability to sense your body's position in space—and we lump senses such as the ability to sense texture and temperature together as "touch" or "feeling."

In any case, for the moment we will focus on two senses: our sight and our hearing. But please bear in mind that everything we say can be applied to our other senses as well, so if you are in a situation where your sense of smell and taste are extremely important (for example, if you are a professional chef), you can apply the same principles.

The Visual Sense

We use our visual sense to take in information through our eyes. This information is then sent to the visual cortex, which lies at the back of the brain. The visual cortex is also used to generate internal images when we use our imagination.

Different Ways of Using the Visual Sense

Evolution was presented with a tricky problem when it was designing the eye because the eye has two main functions.

The first function of the eye is to alert you to danger and opportunity, but especially to danger. On an evolutionary basis, movement represents danger. If something is moving, or at least moving in a purposeful way, it may be alive, and if it's alive, it's potentially dangerous. It's especially dangerous if it is moving toward us, and it is more dangerous if it is moving toward us fast. So one function of the eye is to quickly and accurately identify moving objects and to be able to tell how fast and in what direction they are moving.

The second major function of the eye is to allow you to see detail. For example, as you're reading this book, your eye is making fine distinctions about the shapes of letters, which allow you to read the words.

So you have to be able to quickly and accurately track movement to keep yourself safe from predators, but also be able to see detail so that you can use your intelligence to read books or make tools out of flint or whatever else you *have* to do to survive in the world. At the same time, it's not necessary to see the details of the stripes on the tiger to avoid being eaten, and it's not necessary to track the movement of letters on the page, because they don't move.

The way your eye has dealt with these twin challenges is by delegating each function to a different part of the eye. The task of seeing details is carried out by the fovea. The fovea is a small area around the optic nerve. If you hold your hand out at arm's length and look at your thumbnail, the image will more or less cover the fovea of your eye.

The task of seeing movement is delegated to the rest of your retina around the fovea, an area called the peripheral. This area has a different type of light-sensitive cell that is primarily designed to track movement, even in the dark.

So when your caveman ancestor was walking through the forest, the fovea of his eye was looking out for detail— perhaps small berries that he might be able to eat, while the peripheral was looking out for movement that might mean he was about to be eaten by a saber-toothed tiger.

In fact, evolution went one step further. It not only delegated these two different functions to different parts of the eye, but it also delegated the attention of these two areas to different parts of the brain. So the left hemisphere of your brain was tasked to pay particular attention to the fovea of your eye, while the right hemisphere of your brain was tasked to pay particular attention to the peripheral.

You can think of this as conscious attention and unconscious attention, respectively, if that helps. What this allows you to do is to pay conscious attention to detail—for example, you may be texting on your phone as you walk through the streets—but then to be shocked back to current awareness if you see something moving out of the corner of your eye, perhaps an approaching cyclist.

Exercise

It is quite easy to experience this split attention in practice. Read the instructions for this exercise before you begin.

Go out into the street and find something to look at. For example, you might want to stand on the sidewalk and gaze at a shop window. As you do, notice the details of all the things in the window.

Now, as you continue to look at the details of the things in the window, begin to notice the movement of people around you as they walk past, without looking directly at them. You should find that you are able to do both tasks easily at the same time because they are being carried out by different parts of your brain.

Another interesting phenomenon that is attached to your attention is that your attention is directly linked to your level of stress. You see, when your caveman ancestor noticed a saber-toothed tiger moving in his peripheral vision, he would immediately look straight in the direction of the tiger, meaning the tiger would come into his foveal vision. At the same time, his stress would begin to elevate as his sympathetic nervous system was activated, and he prepared for fight, flight or freeze. But then, if the tiger walked away, he would return to a more open attention, and his level of stress would go down as his parasympathetic nervous system was activated ("rest and digest").

What this means in practice is that if you pay attention to your peripheral vision, you begin to stimulate your parasympathetic nervous system, and your level of stress automatically goes down.

So when you are paying attention to the world around you, it's not just what you're paying attention to, but also how you're paying attention. Are you focusing more on your foveal vision, looking at the detail of something, or are you paying more attention to your peripheral vision, being aware of everything around you?

So, for example, if you're reading a blog, you will be paying attention to foveal vision. But if you are playing basketball, you are probably in peripheral vision.

Sense of Hearing

Exactly the same applies to your sense of hearing. If you are in a one-on-one conversation in a busy room, you will focus on the words your companion is saying. At the same time, your unconscious mind will be paying attention to all the background noise. This is why your attention can be grabbed when you hear your name spoken, even if it's from the far side of the room.

Setting Your Attention in the BEAT

The third step of the BEAT System is "A," for attention. This is not only what you're paying attention to but also how you're paying attention.

Because we spend most of our time reading, or texting, or looking at a computer screen, we spend most of our time in foveal vision. Therefore, you will have the biggest experience if you move into peripheral vision.

Exercise: Anchoring Peripheral Vision

An easy way to go into peripheral vision is to hold your hands up in front of you at arm's length so you can see the backs of your hands. Begin to wiggle your fingers.

Now slowly move your hands apart until they are extended to the sides at shoulder height. As you do so, keep your eyes looking straight ahead but spread your attention out so that you can see both hands at the same time as they spread out. When you do this, your eyes will be in peripheral vision because you can't look directly at both hands at the same time.

Notice at what exact point your hands disappear from your view. Repeat this exercise several times so you get used to going into peripheral vision.

Now spread your attention in the same way, but without using your hands as a guide. Simply look straight ahead, focusing on the point directly in front of you, and then allow your attention to widen, and widen, and widen, until you can see all of the room, all of the space, around you, including the walls, floor, ceiling, and even the space behind you. Practice this until you can do it easily and naturally.

Now we are going to attach this experience to a specific

kinesthetic action, thus creating an anchor. We are beginning to wire together this physical movement with the ability to easily access peripheral vision.

In order to do this, go into peripheral vision once more, and as you do so, press the thumb and ring finger of your right hand together. This is the anchor for "A" in the BEAT. Repeat this process a few times in order to fix this in place, or "condition" the anchor, and then test it. You can test it simply by pressing your thumb and ring finger together and noticing if you immediately access your peripheral vision. If you do, you are ready to move on. If not, just repeat the process a few more times until you begin to notice that you are going into peripheral vision each time.

Chapter 8: Your Thoughts

As human beings, we have the capacity for thought, particularly abstract thought that far exceeds the capacity of any other animal in the known universe. This is what allows us to make tools, from simple flint knives to automobiles to computers to entire cities.

Homo sapiens

As a species, we are known as *Homo sapiens,* meaning "twice wise." One way of interpreting this is to say that we can "think about thinking"; after all, lots of animals think, but as far as we know, no other animal thinks about their own thoughts.

As we discussed in Chapter 2, we think using our senses. We see pictures, we hear sounds, we talk to ourselves, and we have gut feelings. But everything we "think"—at least everything we consciously think—we experience through our internal senses.

Thoughts as Words

Very often, we think in words, for example, "I must do the shopping," "Fred doesn't like me," and so on. This is very powerful because words allow us to turn real-life experiences into abstract experiences that are easier to manipulate. For example, "I must do the shopping" allows us to incorporate the ideas of getting cash out of the ATM, going to the grocery store, gathering certain foods that we buy on a regular basis, browsing for other foods, taking everything to the checkout, paying, carrying everything home, and storing it in the fridge or the cupboards. All this detailed activity is encapsulated by the phrase "do the shopping."

The problem with this type of "thinking in words" is that it takes us out of the moment. We typically think in words about the past or the future rather than the present. It is very difficult to describe the present in words. Think about a sports commentator on the radio. First of all, he has to narrow his attention to one particular part of the activity—typically where the ball is. So first of all, he might describe the baseball pitcher throwing the ball, and then the batter hitting the ball, and then the fielder chasing or catching the ball and throwing it back to the baseman, and so on.

It's very difficult to capture reality in words on a real-time basis. But thinking in words is very powerful for thinking abstractly.

Thinking in the BEAT

Because the purpose of the BEAT System is to enter peak performance states easily "in the moment," as far as possible we will stay away from thinking in words. Instead, we will suggest that you think in pictures using your working memory.

As a reminder, your working memory consists of three parts:

- A short visual loop, or movie screen
- A sound track associated with the movie
- A title for the movie

So what sort of "thoughts" should you have in the moment? Well, there's not a lot of point in thinking about the past while you're living in the moment. At the same time, there's no point in thinking about the present, because you're already tracking the present through your senses, i.e., you're actually seeing and hearing what's going on right now.

The only time left to think about is the future, and that's exactly what you should do. So what we're going to suggest in the BEAT System is that you:

- Think in pictures
- Think about the future

When you make an image about what you want the future to be like, you set up a dissonance within your own brain. You see, your eyes are looking at the present and are presenting you with one picture based on that, while your imagination is thinking about the future and presenting you with another picture based on that. These two pictures are not the same (otherwise the future would be the present!). People who picture the future as being the same as the present are the people who repeat their mistakes. They stay stuck in this loop and are creating their own future based on the present. You may hear your clients say things like: "I've always been this way," "I've always been overweight," "I have always been nervous of speaking in public," and so on.

When your brain is presented with a dissonance, it seeks to

reconcile it. It does this by either trying to make the internal pictures match the present or by trying to make the present match the future. If you can keep a strong internal representation—a picture of how you want the future to be—your brain will try to make the present conform to that.

This Is the Secret of *The Secret*

There are actually several caveats to this approach that we want to stress. These are based on research that indicates that simply engaging in wishful thinking makes it less likely that you will achieve your goals, not more likely. To truly activate the power of your unconscious mind, you should take the following steps, at least with respect to the BEAT System, to take you into a peak performance state in the moment:

1. Imagine a picture of what things will look like in the future, at the end of this specific interaction. So the picture will be set in the same place you are right now, with the same people who are present right now.
2. Make the picture dissociated, meaning that you see yourself in the picture; you are not looking out of your own eyes. The reason for this is that if you strongly imagine seeing out of your own eyes in the future, your unconscious mind may simply assume the future is the present and not try to change the present!
3. Include things that might prevent you from reaching your goal so you can properly address them. For example, if you are in a sales meeting, you might want to visualize objections that your prospects might raise.
4. Add a sound track to the movie.
5. Add a title to the movie that indicates why you want this outcome, i.e., what is important about it to you?

6. Make the picture big, bright, and close for the reasons described below.

So, at the end of this process, you will have a short movie in your mind with a sound track. The movie will have a title that is inspiring and motivating to you. You will see yourself in the movie (you will not be looking out of your own eyes), and the movie will include you overcoming at least one challenge.

Example

Suppose you are in a sales meeting with the CIO of an important client, and you are pitching her on a new computer system.

In terms of your external sensory experience, you will put your attention on your client or prospect. You will look at her and listen to her.

In your thoughts, your internal sensory experience, you will make a movie. The title of the movie might be *Number One Salesman* or something similar. In the movie, you will see yourself and your client. Your client will be raising some kind of objection to the sale, and you'll see yourself masterfully dealing with this, resulting in you and your client agreeing on terms, smiling at each other, and shaking hands.

Your Unconscious Vocabulary

When you think in pictures in this way, your unconscious mind has a specific vocabulary it uses to organize the meaning of the thought. Just as verbs, nouns, and adjectives organize verbal thoughts, this unconscious vocabulary organizes visual thoughts.

In NLP, the elements of this internal vocabulary are called

"submodalities." Submodalities are the qualities of these pictures and sounds that you make inside your own mind. They include things like how big the picture is, how bright the picture is, the location of the picture, and whether the picture is still or moving, framed or unframed, and so on.

In general, the bigger, closer, and brighter a picture is, the more compelling it is. As always, this only applies to positive pictures! If the picture is negative, then big, bright, and close are likely to make you feel more negative!

However, when you make a picture of your outcome, you should make it big, bright, and close. This will make it more compelling to you.

Thoughts ("T") within the BEAT

Once you have constructed an internal movie of your outcome, it's time to anchor it within the BEAT System. To do this, run the movie within your working memory, and when it is just the way you want it to be, make it big and bright and close. Now squeeze your thumb and little finger together. Repeat this several times to anchor this "thought."

Chapter 9: Putting It Together: The BEAT in Practice

In Chapters 5–8, we discussed the basic pieces of the BEAT System step-by-step. Now it is time to put together the pieces we have discussed in previous chapters. We will begin with the Ideal-Self BEAT.

Variation One: The Basic Ideal-Self BEAT System

In the Ideal-Self BEAT, you will model your own ideal self to create the BEAT System.

Begin by finding an open space where you can take four steps forward. These can be small steps—they don't need to be giant strides! Imagine four points on the ground in front of you labeled B-E-A-T. If you wish, you can easily mark the points with four coins or other markers to show you exactly where to step.

Step 1: B

Imagine your ideal self standing on the first of the points. Notice how you're standing with your feet firmly planted on the ground, your weight centered, and your head raised as if it is suspended from a thread hanging from the ceiling. Notice the slow, deep breaths you are taking, the expression on your face, and the look in your eye.

When you're happy with the picture, step forward into the "you" and feel how it feels. Make any adjustments so that it feels just right to you. As you do, squeeze your thumb and forefinger together, and say, "B."

Step 2: E

Imagine your ideal self standing on the next point. Make the picture a little bigger and brighter than the first. Pay particular attention to the look on your face and what that says about your emotional state.

Take a step forward into this ideal self, maintaining your posture. Check inside and notice how you're feeling. You probably find that you're feeling pretty good, in which case you can squeeze your thumb and middle finger together, "E."

If you are not feeling the way you would like, notice where you feel that in your body. Notice the size, shape, and color of the feeling. Simply pay attention to the feeling as a sensation in your body until you notice it beginning to change.

As the feeling changes, ask yourself, "What is important to me about this process, about being my ideal self?" When you find the answer, ask yourself what it's like when you're feeling that value, that quality? Notice where your body feels that.
As you begin to feel a positive feeling, squeeze your thumb and middle finger together and say "E."

Step 3: A

Imagine your ideal self standing on the next point. Make this picture even bigger and even brighter than the previous one. Take a step forward into this third ideal self, maintaining your posture and feeling those good feelings inside.

Allow yourself to go into peripheral vision and peripheral hearing. As you do so, squeeze your thumb and ring finger together, saying "A."

Step 4: T

Imagine your ideal self standing on the next point. Make this picture the biggest and brightest of the four. Take a step forward into this ideal self, maintaining your posture and good feelings and staying in peripheral vision.

Allow the movie of how you want this situation to go to begin playing in your mind. See yourself easily dealing with any obstacles and reaching your goal. As you do so, squeeze your thumb and little finger together and say "T."

Repeat from the beginning to condition the pattern.

Variation Two: Slow-Motion BEAT

In the slow-motion BEAT, we're going to do the Ideal-Self BEAT described above, but this time in slow motion. By slow motion, we mean as slow as humanly possible so that each step you make will take perhaps five to ten seconds to complete. There is something about moving in slow motion that catches the attention of the unconscious mind.
Simply follow the steps in the above variation, but slow everything down by a factor of five or ten!

Variation Three: The Real-Time BEAT

In the Real-Time BEAT, you can use the pattern in the moment to check in, and adjust, how you are "being" in any moment in time. In most situations, you will be able to use the kinesthetic anchors, squeezing your thumb and fingers together one by one. If you're in a situation where you can't do this, you can use the auditory anchors by saying to yourself, "B-E-A-T."

When you are in a situation and you realize that it is not going quite the way you want, take a very brief time-out to run this pattern. It only needs to take a few seconds, so you can do it while you are listening to someone else speak or even during a pause in your own speech.

Step 1: B

Fire the first anchor (your thumb and forefinger, or say the letter "B"), and as you do so, check in with your body, with your physiology. Are your feet comfortably grounded on the floor? Is your weight centered? Is your head raised, as if suspended from a silver cord? If not, make any adjustments you need to make to become grounded, centered, and elongated in the spine.

Step 2: E

Fire the second anchor and check in with how you feel. If you don't feel the way you would like to feel, check where in your body you're feeling that. Notice the size, shape and color, and allow it to begin to change. As it changes, refire the second anchor, and you should move into your positive state.

Step 3: A

Fire the third anchor. As you do this, notice where your attention is. Adjust your attention, if necessary, by moving into peripheral vision and then wrapping your attention around whatever is important in the context.

Step 4: T

Fire the fourth anchor as you notice any thoughts, including any pictures or movies, you are running in your mind. If necessary, bring your thoughts back to seeing your positive outcome and seeing yourself dealing with any obstacles to achieve that outcome.

Variation Four: Deep Trance Identification (DTI) BEAT

The Deep Trance Identification involves "becoming" someone who is highly skilled in the activity you wish to do (please see our book *Deep Trance Identification* by Shawn Carson and Jess Marion with John Overdurf, available from Amazon.com, for details). For simplicity we will be using the female pronoun though out this example.

This technique requires some preparation. At a minimum, you need to be able to picture your model within your mind's eye, including posture, breathing, facial expression, and gestures. You also need to understand, or at least have some insight into, your model's emotional states when she is performing at her best, as well as what your model is paying attention to and what she is thinking.

Before you begin, find a space where you can take four small steps forward. Imagine four marks on the floor in front of you, labeled B-E-A-T.

Step 1: B

See your model standing on the first point on the floor, the one labeled "B." Notice how your model is standing and breathing as well as her facial expression and gestures. If your model is smaller than you, make the picture big enough to step into.

Now step into the model and take on one aspect of her physiology, perhaps a gesture or facial expression. Allow that one thing to lead you into the rest of your model's physiology.

Squeeze your thumb and forefinger together, "B."

Step 2: E

See a new image of your model standing on the second point, the one labeled "E." In particular, notice your model's facial expression as a window into her emotions. Step forward into the model, adopting her facial expression.

Notice how you're feeling inside; this is your current state. If you're not feeling the way you want, ask yourself what's important about doing this deep trance identification. Once you have found that value, ask yourself what it's like when you're living that value. You will begin to feel a positive, resourceful feeling inside that arises from that value.

Squeeze your thumb and middle finger together, "E."

Step 3: A

See a third image of your model standing on the third point, the one labeled "A." In particular, notice your model's gaze, where she is looking, and whether she is looking with a focused or a more diffuse view. Step forward into the model, adopting the expression in her eyes.

Notice what you're paying attention to and how you're paying attention. Squeeze your thumb and ring finger together, "A."

Step 4: T

See a fourth image of your model standing on the fourth point, the one labeled "T." Notice your model's facial expression once more, this time as a window into her thoughts. Step forward into the model, adopting that facial expression.

Notice what you're thinking. Squeeze your thumb and pinky together, "T."

Section 3:

The BEAT System in Practice

Chapter 10: Practical Aspects of the BEAT

In the next section, we talk about how to do the BEAT System in practice. We'll walk you through a number of ways of using the BEAT in different contexts.

This is by no means intended to be an exhaustive list of all the times and places where you can use the BEAT System, but rather a series of examples that will lead you to generalize the BEAT in your life. When you've seen any system applied enough times, your unconscious mind begins to "own" it, so to speak, and you find that you're able to use it easily, anytime and anyplace.

So please feel free to pick one of the applications and dive into that chapter. Get the BEAT literally under your fingertips and weave it into your physiology, feeling great knowing you have those skills and looking for opportunities to put them into practice.

But before you go running off all fired up to transform your life in wonderful and unexpected ways, we will give you a few preliminary tips.

Preparing for the BEAT

The first suggestion we would like to make is based on the important distinction between practice and performance. A professional athlete would never consider stepping onto the playing field without practicing first—and practicing, and practicing, and practicing, until the skill was second nature.

So first of all, pick a quiet time and place to practice—a time when you will not be disturbed. Once you have integrated the BEAT, you can practice it in a matter of seconds, but for the first few times through, you should give yourself at least ten or fifteen minutes to practice.

You'll find it easier to practice if you have a practice partner lead you through the steps. While he or she is focusing on the steps, you can focus on your physiology, your emotional state, your sensory awareness, and your thoughts.

If you don't have a practice partner, you might want to record the instructions and play them back on your iPod or recording device as you practice.

Choosing a Context

Choose a particular time and place where you want to be different from how you are now. Where specifically will you be? What day of the week will this take place and at what time of day? What or who will you see when you're there?

Now ask yourself, "How do I want to be different in this specific context?" What will it look like when you are? How will you be feeling? Will the BEAT that you have installed lead you to this outcome?

Practicing the BEAT

Once you've chosen a quiet time and place, and ideally have a practice partner, it's time to actually begin practicing. Take the steps one at a time, B-E-A-T, spending enough time on each step that you are comfortable with it.

Remember to use spatial, kinesthetic, and auditory anchors for each step.

As soon as the steps seem easy and natural, begin to run them as a sequence, B-E-A-T. Then take a short break for a few seconds and once again run the sequence, B-E-A-T.

You can run the sequence as many times as you want, with one caveat. If you begin to feel bored with the exercise, you must stop. After all, boredom is an emotional state, and if you do the BEAT while you are bored, you will simply anchor boredom rather than the emotional state of "confidence" or whatever else you are seeking to feel.

Installing the BEAT

Now that you've got the BEAT at your fingertips and you have a particular context in which you are going to use it, you want to install it. Installing the BEAT System will make it automatic within the context you have chosen.

There are two methods that we are going to use to install the BEAT:
- Future pacing
- Using contextual anchors together with the NLP Swish pattern

Future Pacing

Future pacing simply refers to the mental rehearsal of a

skill.

What you're going to do is to imagine you are in the specific context you chose earlier. In your mind's eye, see who and what you see there, and hear what you hear.

When you can fully imagine being there, run through the four steps of the BEAT that you have already practiced, B-E-A-T. Now, blank your internal movie screen and start again, seeing who and what you will see, hearing what you will hear, and firing off the four anchors, B-E-A-T.

Repeat this process until you are absolutely comfortable using the BEAT System in this imaginary context.

The Swish Pattern

The Swish pattern allows you to anchor the BEAT onto the specific context you've chosen. What you'll do is to choose something that you naturally see within that context and use that as the trigger for the BEAT; we will call this the trigger image. For example, you might want to use the door you will have to step through to get into the room where the action will take place.

Once you have this image, it's time to do the Swish pattern. You want to take the image of your ideal self, shrink it down temporarily until it is the size of a postage stamp, and stick it onto the trigger image.

Now, as you imagine seeing the trigger image with the postage stamp-sized picture of your ideal self stuck onto it, imagine that ideal "you" bursting out so it becomes a three-dimensional, life-size, big, bright, and powerful image of your ideal self in front of you.

As soon as you see this, step forward into this ideal "you," adopting that ideal physiology, squeezing your thumb and forefinger together… "B." Now run through the rest of the pattern, E-A-T.

Now blank your internal movie screen and repeat the Swish: see the trigger image with the postage stamp-sized picture of your ideal self. Your ideal self bursts out so it's big, bright, life-size, and three-dimensional. Step into that ideal self, adopting that physiology and firing off the first trigger… "B." Then continue with the rest of the sequence, E-A-T. Repeat, repeat, repeat, until every time you see the trigger image, that ideal "you" leaps out, and you find yourself pulled forward into it, B-E-A-T.

Generalizing the BEAT

Once you have the BEAT automatically at your fingertips in one context, you will want to begin generalizing it to other similar contexts.

You might want to start by imagining the same place but at a different time. Perhaps you have to give a presentation at work every Monday morning; the first context might be on Monday of the following week, the second context on Monday of the week after that, and so on.

Then you might want to generalize to another place. Perhaps you also have to give presentations at your client's office. So you might want to extend it to a specific time when you expect this to happen.

Stress Testing the BEAT

Now that you've installed the BEAT in several locations and several times, you might want to begin to stress test it.

You can do this by imagining what might go wrong in each of the contexts immediately after you have fired off the B-E-A-T anchors. Returning to the example of giving presentations, imagine you are in the office, you have fired off the B-E-A-T, and you suddenly find that your PowerPoint slides won't load on the computer. How do you deal with that, now?

If, and to the extent that, you find your physiology changing for the worse, or feel your heart drop into your stomach, or maybe your gaze becomes fixated on your computer screen rather than on your clients, or your brain starts to run a negative thought loop ("Oh my God, what am I going to do now?!!!"), you have some more work to do on the BEAT.

If you find this happening a lot, you probably want to install the Recovery BEAT described in Chapter 16.

Practice Makes Perfect

With the BEAT System, it really is a case of practice makes perfect. Repetition is key. The more times you practice the BEAT, the more likely it will be there when you need it.

If you get the opportunity, you might want to practice it in the actual context where you will be using it. For example, if you're giving a presentation and you have an opportunity beforehand to visit the stage or room where you will be giving the presentation, practicing the BEAT in the actual place where you will need it will be hugely beneficial.

Chapter 11: Sensory Filters

How much information are you exposed to at any point in time? It turns out that this is an enormously difficult question to answer because it depends so much upon how you measure it. For example, if you think about your eyes, should you count the photons of light that are entering them at any moment in time? Or perhaps you should count the number of rods and cones (light-sensitive cells) in each eye, or perhaps the capacity of your optic nerves to carry signals back to your brain.

The highest number of bits of information I have seen estimated as being available to us at any point in time is forty-two million. Other estimates are lower than this, but certainly all the estimates I have seen are in the millions.

How many pieces of information can we consciously track at any one point in time? The standard answer to this question is seven plus or minus two, i.e., somewhere between five and nine pieces of information at any one time. More modern research indicates that the number may actually be much lower and that we have significant trouble tracking two pieces of information at once!

So somehow we have to take up to forty-two million bits of information and distill them down into the most important seven pieces of information. This is quite a task for your brain to do in an optimal manner!

Those people who fail to achieve their goals often do so because they are paying attention to the wrong pieces of information. For example, think about the poor, unfortunate man who believes that, "I can't do this. I'm no good at anything." His unconscious mind takes this as an instruction to sort for sensory information that supports this thought. As a result, he's going to see everything that just went wrong for him. Leaving aside the emotional pain that this can cause, it also tends to block all the information that would actually be useful!

This is the way in which your unconscious mind sets the "filters" that it uses to determine which of the forty-two million bits of information get presented to your conscious mind. Your unconscious mind uses your beliefs and values to select the "right" information to show you. For example, research has shown that people who consider themselves to be "lucky" tend to see opportunities that come their way, while those who consider themselves to be "unlucky" miss these same opportunities.

Therefore, if someone has "bad" filters, such as believing they are a failure, their unconscious mind will tend to:
- Show them and remind them of events in which they failed. As we know, these negative thoughts will tend to lead to negative emotions, which in turn will tend to lead to an un-resourceful physiology.
- Filter out, and therefore not show them, opportunities that could lead to their success.

In contrast, if someone has "good" filters, such as believing they are skillful, their unconscious mind will tend to:

- Filter out, and therefore not show them, information that is irrelevant to their goals.
- Show them opportunities to succeed.

Setting "Good" Filters

As we have seen, filters are vital for sorting through the forty-two million bits of information that are available to you at any one time. So it's important to know how to set filters that are going to help you achieve your goals.

There are several different types of filters, for example, beliefs, values, and memories. We don't have time to go through each of these in detail or cover how to best remove the old filters and set new, empowering filters. Instead, we will offer you a shortcut that will allow you to quickly and easily set positive filters that will help you achieve specific goals.

The simplest way to do this is using a technique you already know, namely the T = Thoughts of the BEAT System. Essentially, this involves seeing what you will be seeing when you have achieved your goal.

In the BEAT System, you set your perceptual filters by imagining, within your mind's eye, exactly what you will be seeing when you have succeeded in your purpose or goal within the context you are stepping into.

Imagining your immediate short-term goal in this way sets your filters using a process called neurological priming. Research into priming shows that even the subtlest of markers can have significant effects on how we process information. For example, in one experiment, participants were asked to solve a word-search puzzle containing words linked to either patience or impatience. One group of participants had to find words such as *yield, polite*, and *courteous*. The other group had to find words such as *bold, rude*, and *bother*. At the end of the word search, the participants were asked to hand their papers in to the researcher. Now, unbeknownst to the participants, the finding of the set words was not the main focus of the test—the "handing in the paper" was. Because, you see, the researchers had set it up so that the person accepting the papers was deep in conversation with another member of the research team, and the participant had to wait awhile in order to hand in his or her paper. The results were fascinating. Those people who had been asked to focus on the "impatient" group of words were much quicker to interrupt the conversation in order to hand in their paper. In contrast, the participants who had been primed with words related to patience showed much more patience themselves.

Let's do a simple experiment so that you can experience priming for yourself. Take a moment and think of the color red, see the color in your mind's eye (it may help to close your eyes for a moment), say the word, *red, red, red*. Now look around the room… Chances are you will notice things that are red. Now repeat the experiment with blue… In each case, you will likely find that your eyes become sensitized to the color, and they filter for objects of that color as you look around.

In this case, we are seeking to set wider filters that will be useful over a range of contexts. When you can do this, your unconscious mind will always be on the lookout for opportunities that will advance you toward your goals.

Setting Goal-Based Filters

You can set wider, goal-based filters using a simple two-step process.

The first step is similar to the BEAT process discussed above. Within the context of your goal, you imagine what your future will be like when you have achieved your goal. For example, if your goal is to get a promotion at work, perhaps you imagine being in the corner office and sitting at your new desk. Notice something in the context that tells you when it is taking place, for example, your calendar or phone with today's date.

Probably the most famous example of this strategy is Jim Carrey, the comic actor. Carrey tells the story of how he used to carry around a check for one million dollars. This represented his promise to himself for his future.

The second step is extremely important. When you construct the first picture, it should be as if you are seeing out of your own eyes. You should now step out of that picture so you can see yourself in the picture (like a photo or a movie that someone else filmed). You should then take this second picture and place it in your future. For most people, the future is on their right and/or in front of them. Put the picture in your future so you can see yourself achieving the goal at that future date.

The reason this second step is so important is that if you simply imagine that you have already achieved your goal, research shows it actually robs you of motivation. It is as if your unconscious mind actually believes you have already achieved the goal and stops trying. For example, a group of college students were asked to imagine that they were acing a test. As a result, their grades actually went down; they felt so good about their chances in the test that they stopped studying for it!

So to recap, step into the experience of having achieved your goals and feel good about that, then step out of that experience and put the photo or movie into your future. This gives your unconscious mind something to work toward.

Chapter 12: Achieving Excellence

Keys to Excellence

There are several keys to achieving excellence in your life.

These are:
1. Knowing what you want
2. Taking action toward what you want
3. Knowing if those actions are moving you in the right direction, toward your goal
4. Having the flexibility to change course if necessary
5. Having the resiliency to keep going when things get tough

If you have all five of these qualities, you are sure to eventually achieve your goals! And using the BEAT System will make your dreams come true much sooner than otherwise!

However, if you lack any one of these qualities, you might never achieve your goals. You might spend your life chasing things you don't really want, or not taking the actions you need to take in order to achieve your dreams, or doing things that are counterproductive and that move you even further away from the things you do want, or perhaps doing the same old things even though they are not working, or simply giving up when things get tough. So although the BEAT System is an awesome tool, if you don't know the direction in which you are moving or what your goals are, it is useless to you.

Because this is a book about the BEAT System, not about goal setting, we are not going to go into too much depth on goals and how to achieve your dreams. But because knowing where you are going is so important, we have included this chapter to provide an overview of how to set your goals, how to take action, how to measure your results, and how to build flexibility and resiliency.

Knowing What You Want

Do you know what you want? How do you know that you want it? What would it look like if you had it? Do you really care? What might you have to give up in order to achieve it, and if you do have to give something up, is it really worthwhile?

The sad fact is that most people can't answer these questions. They don't really know what they want, or they can't describe what it would look like if they had it. Or perhaps they know what they want, but it's not important enough to them to sacrifice what they have to sacrifice in order to get it.

Some people have no goals at all. They spend their lives stuck in dead-end jobs, thinking to themselves, "Is this all there is?" They don't have what they want in life because they don't know what it is they want.

Other people have goals that have nothing to do with who they are or what's really important to them. Perhaps they want to become movie stars but have no interest in learning the craft of acting. They just want to be famous for the sake of being famous. When asked why they want to be famous, they talk about wealth and status and being recognized in the street.

Don't misunderstand this—there is nothing wrong with wanting to be famous for the sake of being famous as long as you recognize that that's what you really want! Knowing what you really want gives you options for achieving it. In these days of YouTube, plenty of people are famous for nothing more than putting up interesting or amusing videos on the Internet. It is certainly not easy to get a YouTube channel with a million subscribers, but it is certainly a lot easier than becoming a famous movie star.

Still other people have goals that they are genuinely attracted to, but they don't actually undertake the boring and mundane tasks required to achieve those goals. For example, someone might want to be a musician, and they might genuinely love playing music. But they might not be prepared to put in the time to practice the technical skills they need in order to become a great musician. There is a disconnect in their mind between these boring tasks and their dreams.

Some people know exactly what they want and are prepared to take action toward it, but they are either oblivious to the fact that those actions are not working or too inflexible to change what they are doing. I was recently consulting for a company where one of the employees wanted a pay raise. He approached his boss but was turned down. Rather than asking what he would have to do to get the raise, he instead complained bitterly to anyone and everyone in the company about his boss and how badly he had been treated. It took no time at all for his behavior to be reported back to his boss, and not only did he not get his pay raise, but he very nearly got fired in the bargain. He was either too oblivious to realize the effects of his behavior or too inflexible to do anything else.

Big Dreams and Little Goals

It's great to dream big. If you want to change the world, you'd better have a big dream! The bigger the dream, the more energy it gives you to move forward. Supercoach Tony Robbins often asked his clients, "If you could wake up in the morning knowing that anything is possible, what would you do?" Take a moment to answer this question for yourself before you read on.

Once you have your dream, you need to give it energy. To give a dream the energy it needs to propel you forward, you need to put it on the big movie screen of your mind.

Exercise

Read all the instructions before you begin.

Imagine you have already achieved your dream. Where are you? What are you seeing? What are you hearing that lets you know you've achieved your dream? Perhaps you're on the stage at Carnegie Hall having just finished your piano solo...

Whatever your dream is, imagine sitting in a movie theater watching yourself on the screen. You've just achieved your big dream! Congratulations! What do you see?

If you want, you can edit the movie to make it even better. After all, you are the director of your own life.

Now step (or float) into that movie. Step into that specific time and place when you've achieved your dream. Feel what that's like from the inside!

Now step out of the movie and back into the movie theater. Now open your eyes and come back to the here and now.

Now, let me ask you a question: how do you feel about your achievement? If you feel awesome and amazing, that's all well and good. But if you feel a little deflated, perhaps your dream is the wrong one for you. Let's take an example that we all see regularly played out in the tabloid press: you dream of being a movie star! Now imagine walking down the streets of New York with your gorgeous spouse... surrounded by the flash of cameras from the pursuing paparazzi. Many stars who thought they wanted fame found out that it's not always such a good thing!

So when you put yourself inside your dream, think about all the things you may lose as well as everything you'll gain!

You have your dream—now you have to turn it into a series of actions. These actions should be specific mini-goals that are entirely under your control. We will talk more about how to do this in the section "Taking Action."

Stating It in the Positive

If you've been doing the exercises, the following comments are going to seem pretty obvious to you.

You should state your goal in the positive. This means you should say what you want, not what you don't want. Why is this? It's simple—it's impossible for your unconscious mind to make a picture of that kind of goal without first making a picture of what you don't want! Let's say you're playing golf, and you say to yourself, "Don't slice the ball into the trees." The only way your unconscious mind can make sense of this instruction is to—you guessed it—first make a picture of you slicing the ball into the trees and then putting a line through this picture or something else that indicates it's what you don't want.

The better approach is to state your goal in the positive by saying what you do want: "I want to drive the ball to the middle of the fairway just where that light patch of grass is." Your unconscious mind is then able to make a movie of the outcome that you do actually want.

Being Specific

In the same way, and for the same reason, your goals should be as specific as possible. If you simply said to yourself, "I want to drive the ball to the middle of the fairway," you may find yourself miss-striking the ball and sending it only ten yards, but right in the middle of the fairway. You got exactly what you asked for.

The simplest way to make your goals specific, especially short-term mini-goals, is to visualize exactly what you want to see. This is why you should visualize your specific outcome under the "T" of the BEAT System.

Flexibility and Resiliency

Flexibility means the ability to change what you are doing when you realize that what you are doing is not working.

Resiliency is the ability to overcome setbacks, as Chumbawamba said in their 1997 hit song "Tubthumping": "I get knocked down but I get up again."

The Key to Flexibility

The key to flexibility is to stay in the moment. It is wonderful to make plans about what you intend to do, but those plans will not survive their first contact with reality. Something will be different from how you thought it would be.

By staying in the moment, you allow your mind to continually update your plans—to reconfigure to what is happening now. This requires that you constantly ask yourself the questions, "What just happened, and what should I do now as a result of that?"

Of course, this requires you to be able to answer this question. Being able to choose an action as a result of what just happened requires one key resource: experience. If you have sufficient experience, you will always be able to do something appropriate within the situation. No matter what happens, you will have a response.

There is a popular meme that says you need ten thousand hours of experience to master a skill. It doesn't mean that you will necessarily master a skill after ten thousand hours of experience, but rather that you will not be a true master until you have at least those ten thousand hours of experience. To give you a guide, ten thousand hours represent around five years of full-time work.

We can't give you experience within your chosen field (unless you want to sign up for all of our courses). But we can give you an invaluable hint, which is this: when you think about the specific context in which you are going to use the BEAT System, imagine being in that context, and imagine all the things that could happen and what your response would be.

It's like the movie *Groundhog Day*. Bill Murray is a TV weatherman who gets to live the same day over and over again until he gets it perfectly right. He can test his behaviors in the real world, knowing that he can always try again tomorrow.

By running these experiences within your imagination, you get to experience anything and everything the world might throw at you, and you get to practice how you might respond to each of these.

Resiliency

Resiliency is a prerequisite for flexibility. Resiliency means being able to pick yourself up off the ground whenever life knocks you down, stand up again, and try something new.

The story that best illustrates the concept of resiliency for us is from Thomas Edison. After his thousandth attempt to make a functioning light bulb, Edison was asked how it felt to have failed a thousand times. Edison replied that he had not failed a thousand times, he had not even failed once, and in fact he had discovered a thousand ways to not make a light bulb.

This may sound like just a clever way to get out of an embarrassing question. In fact, Thomas Edison was quite serious in his answer. Edison learned from each of the experimental light bulbs he had made. By noticing the precise way in which each of the filaments burned out in these experiments, Edison identified an electromagnetic phenomenon that he called the Edison Effect. The Edison Effect was what allowed Edison to create electronic tubes that ultimately led to the invention of radio and television. That is quite some failure!

When you are able to view each interaction you have with the world around you as an experiment that gets you one step closer to your goal, irrespective of the result, there will truly be no failure—there will only be feedback. When you view everything that happens as feedback in your mindset and behavior, you will have mastered the art of resiliency.

Taking Action

The only way you will achieve your goals and reach your dreams is if you take action toward them. Here are a few techniques to help you take the actions necessary to move toward your goals.

Technique One: Making a Commitment to Yourself

One of the most powerful methods you can use to provide the motivation to take the next step toward your goal is to make a commitment to do so. There are a number of ways you can do this. The simplest way is to actually set written short-term goals for yourself. These goals should be in the form of specific actions you will take—things that are within your specific control.

Research indicates that the biggest predictor of who will achieve the goals they want in life is simply based upon who writes these goals down, looks at them, and reviews them on a regular basis.

So, for example, you set a goal of running a marathon next year. That's fantastic, but you are much more likely to achieve that goal if you write it down.

So, let's assume you set a goal of running a marathon next year, and you write that down. That's fantastic, but you're much more likely to achieve that goal if you look at it, think about it, and update it on a regular basis.

Let's assume that on Monday, you set a goal of running a marathon next year. You write that down. On Tuesday, you look at it, think about it, and realize that not only have you not achieved it yet, but you haven't taken any steps toward achieving it. You still like the goal of running a marathon next year, but now it's Tuesday—time to update it. So you set a goal of getting off the bus one stop earlier than usual and walking the last half mile home so you begin to exercise in order to be able to run the marathon next year.

Now it's Wednesday. You got off the bus one stop earlier yesterday and walked the last half mile home. Congratulations. Now it's time to update your goal, so you set a goal of jogging around the park three times a week before you go to work in the morning. On your way home on Wednesday, you get off the bus one stop early and walk the last half mile home. On Thursday, you wake up forty-five minutes earlier and jog around the park. Now it's time to update your goal again.

Once you get in the habit of constantly writing down, taking action toward, achieving, and updating your goals, success becomes the inevitable outcome.

Technique Two: Making a Commitment to Others

The second way in which you can make a commitment is to make a commitment to others. For example, you can tell your friends and family that you intend to achieve a certain goal by a certain date. You can also tell your colleagues at work, and even your enemies, because this will really make you want to do what you said you were going to do!

You can even post your intention on Facebook or join one of the Internet coaching groups that allow you to make a public commitment to your goals.

In fact, you can tell everyone! Of course, if you were the sort of person who found it easy to break these types of commitments, it wouldn't do you any good to make the commitments in the first place. But as we know, you're not that sort of person, so making these commitments will certainly help you.

Technique Three: No Zero Days

"No zero days" is a meme that you will find on the Internet. We're not sure who started it, but it's a very useful tool that fits in well with the idea of writing down and continuously updating goals.

No zero days means that each and every day, you take some action toward your goal. It can be a very small action that takes only five or ten minutes, or you may dedicate the entire day to it. Whatever it is that you do, the important thing is that you do something.

If you follow the concept of no zero days, you begin to strengthen your willpower as well as make daily progress toward your goals.

The benefit of this approach is that you never need to feel overwhelmed because on any one day, you can take a very small action if that's all you have the time or energy to do. At the same time, each of these small actions is a success that on some level will make you feel good—make you feel that you are achieving something. This sense of achievement will provide you with more energy toward that goal.

Think of it this way: if you set a huge goal, it is rather like rolling a boulder up a mountain. The very thought of working on that goal seems overwhelming. It becomes easy to say to yourself, "I'm too busy today to do that" or "I'm tired—I'll do it tomorrow." And the more times you say this, and the more times you take a day off, the steeper the mountain becomes.

But if you take some small action and achieve some mini-goal every day, that success adds energy and momentum to the goal. The boulder begins to roll downhill. Perhaps one day you take that action in the morning, and you realize you have the rest of the day in front of you, so you set a second small goal and immediately achieve that, so you set a third goal, and so on. Pretty soon, you're breezing through three or four goals each and every day. And before you know it, you find yourself on top of the mountain.

Use the tools of making a commitment to yourself, making a commitment to others, and no zero days, and you will be amazed at what you can achieve.

Chapter 13: Troubleshooting

In this chapter, we will cover common mistakes and issues that you or your clients may experience when using the BEAT System and how to address them.

Issue 1

I was in a high-stress situation and tried to use the BEAT, but it just didn't work for me.

The BEAT is an anchoring pattern that, on one level, uses classical conditioning. Remember Pavlov and his dogs: Pavlov did not come up with his theory of classical conditioning, then grab a stray dog off the street so he could demonstrate his theory to the scientific community. He took his dogs and conditioned the response first before demonstrating it.

Similarly, you have to condition the BEAT before you step into the situation in which you need it. When you practice the BEAT several times in a relaxed, no-stress situation, your peak state will be available when you need it.

Practice, practice, practice.

Issue 2

I'm not sure I'm stepping into my peak physiology...

Unfortunately, in the modern world, many of us are simply not used to using our physical body. Many people spend their days hunched over a computer screen doing terrible things to their posture! Unless you do some kind of regular exercise that forces you to pay attention to your own physiology on a daily basis, your brain basically forgets how to stand or walk efficiently.

The easiest way to address this is to begin to do some form of regular exercise that allows you to begin to pay attention to your own body—your posture, physiology, movement, and breathing. Disciplines such as tai chi or yoga, or formal dancing such as tango, or simply the walking meditation described in Chapter 17 can help with this. If in doubt, you should consult your medical practitioner before beginning any exercise regime.

In the short term, you can pay attention to your physiology and your breathing. This may not create your "peak" physiology, but it will give you a good starting point. To align your physiology, pay attention to the feeling of your feet on the ground. Now pay attention to your center of gravity—the point in the middle of your belly about three inches below your navel. Finally, pay attention to the crown of your head and imagine it is attached to the sky by a thread. Paying attention to *ground, center, crown* and then *crown, center, ground* will begin to train your body to properly realign itself.

At the same time, you can begin to improve your breathing using the "belly breathing" method described in Chapter 17.

Issue 3

Even after I step into my peak physiology, as soon as I check in with my emotions I feel bad, even after I use the self-coaching pattern.

As we have discussed, this is unusual because stepping into a peak physiology generally feels good! If not, there may be any one of several causes. Here are two of the most common:

1. Your physiology (body and breathing) is still a reflection of this negative state. Perhaps you're still hunched over or have shallow "chest" breathing. A good way to check is to ask a friend to take a look at your physiology and tell you whether or not it looks "resourceful" (or confident, or whatever state you are aiming for).

2. You are running negative movies in your working memory or a negative sound track (typically negative self-talk). You may or may not be aware of these negative movies or negative self-talk. To heighten your awareness of your internal mental processes, you can simply ask yourself, "What movies am I making inside my mind, or what am I saying to myself right now, that is making me feel this way?" If you simply allow yourself to sit with this question for a while, the answer will likely present itself.

The most direct way of dealing with negative movies or self-talk (thoughts) within the BEAT, once they are identified, is by using the self-coaching pattern. Put your attention onto the feeling within your body, noticing where it is, whether it has a color or movement, and so on. While you are doing this, it becomes very difficult for you to also run negative movies inside your head, so the negative feeling will leave your body, allowing you to choose a better feeling.

Now, of course you may be dealing with something that is particularly stressful—either a negative memory or some upcoming stressful event. If this is the case, your unconscious mind may be running active movies about this event and may not be prepared to let them go. Your unconscious mind may be telling you that you need to prepare for something in the future such as taking a test or exam. This is an important message, and you should take it seriously! Knowing that you are properly prepared for this future event will ease the worries.

On the other hand, if you're bothered by some particularly difficult and worrisome memory or irrational fear that you cannot let go of, you may want to seek help from a qualified coach or mental health professional (depending upon the nature of the issue).

Issue 4

I'm feeling pretty good doing the BEAT, but I just don't know what I should be focusing my attention on.

The first possibility in this case is that there is a technical skill that you do not yet have. For example, if you are using the BEAT for performance in a sport you are just learning, you may not know how much of your attention to place on the ball, versus the opposing players, versus the goal. If it is this sort of issue, you can, of course, get specific coaching in that skill.

On the other hand, you may be using the BEAT to improve a less specific skill such as creativity. Perhaps there is no one to coach you in this skill, so what do you do?

The first question to ask yourself is, "Am I getting the results I want in this context?" If the answer to this question is yes, you are probably putting your attention on the right things.

On the other hand, if you are not getting the results you want, you are probably putting your attention on the wrong things, even if you're not sure what the right things are!

There is a saying in coaching that if you always do what you've always done, you will always get what you always got. You could rephrase this as: if you always see what you've always seen, you'll always get what you always got.

You can try the following and see what happens; you may have to try the pattern several times to discover what works best for you within your specific context.

- Imagine you are in the context and notice what you are paying attention to.
- Make a mental note to yourself: "Paying attention to that doesn't seem to be working!"
- Go into peripheral vision.
- Ask yourself the question, "What have I not been paying attention to that, when I do, will give me the answer?"
- Allow your attention to settle on something—anything—that you were not paying attention to before.
- Notice how your behaviors, the behaviors of those around you, and the results you obtain change as a result of paying attention to this new thing.
- If you are now getting the results you want, fantastic! If not, repeat the above steps.

This may sound like a pretty random way of getting results, and in many ways it is. Remember that sometimes the biggest breakthroughs come by paying attention to the information that appears to be unrelated to the problem. Charles Darwin developed the theory of evolution by paying attention to the different shapes of finches' beaks!

Issue 5

I keep having negative thoughts and running negative movies in my mind.

Let's say this upfront: there is absolutely nothing wrong with running negative movies in your mind. This only becomes a problem if you allow these to stop you from living the life you want to live.

There is a part of your brain specifically designed to run worst-case scenarios. This has two important evolutionary functions:

- It prevents you from putting yourself in a situation where you would face mortal danger, such as walking into a lion's den.
- It allows you to plan for contingencies.

If you're walking alone at night through the worst neighborhood in town and you suddenly decide to take your wallet out and count your money, that potential falls under the category of putting you in mortal danger. Your unconscious mind is quite right in running negative movies of you being mugged, and you should listen to those movies and act accordingly!

Fortunately, there are very few scenarios in our lives now that place us in mortal danger other than texting on your smartphone while crossing the street or while driving (do not do either one—they are dangerous!). So many of the negative movies you may run in your mind have more to do with allowing you to plan for contingencies. "What could go wrong, and what will I do if it does?"

The trick is to do this contingency planning before you step into the real context. Imagine being in the context and visualizing what could go wrong and how you will respond appropriately if it does. The more scenarios you can imagine inside your imagination, the better prepared you will be for the real thing.

Then when you actually step into the context and practice maintaining that picture or movie of how you want things to look at the end of your interaction, it acts as a "magnet" pulling you toward the optimal outcome. It is this image of success that guides your unconscious mind.

Section 4:

Applications of the BEAT System

Chapter 14: The BEAT System for Coaching

In this chapter, we will discuss using the BEAT System in a coaching context. In previous chapters of the book, we have referred to the coaching BEAT, and even demonstrated it, but in this chapter we will give a specific protocol for using it.

Before you begin teaching the BEAT to your client, you might want to run through the BEAT yourself to put yourself in your peak coaching state. We typically use the following BEAT System to step into our own ideal coaching state:

Body and Breathing

Your physiology is centered and relaxed. The center of your physiological attention is on the central point three inches below the navel.

You might also want to practice heart breathing, allowing your breath to enter your body through your heart and fill up your heart with each breath. This is a spiritual method of breathing that goes back to the medieval monks who would wander into the desert to meditate. It is also described in great depth in the "Heartmath" method.

Emotional State

A big mistake that a lot of coaches make is to "feel sorry" for their clients. A better coaching state is one of lighthearted compassion. As Richard Bandler says, this stuff is way too important to take seriously.

Another useful state is that of deep curiosity—a true interest in the unique individual you will be working with, a fascination with how the client is doing the problem, and a keen interest in expanding his or her possibilities.

Awareness and Attention

There's a specific type of awareness and attention that is ideal for coaching. We call it the "coaching bubble." To experience the coaching bubble, simply go into peripheral vision while you are sitting in front of a partner and looking at him or her. You should be able to see your partner, but you also see the rest of the room behind and around him or her. Continuing to look at your partner, notice that you can put your attention over toward the far left of your visual field or move it to the far right of your visual field without moving your head or your eyes. This is because your attention is different from where you are looking. Once you have the idea of moving your attention around within your visual field, bring your attention in so that it "wraps around" your partner. It should feel as if you and your partner are together within an energetic bubble.

This state's attention will allow you to see all the gestures and movements that your partner makes. This is powerful information for you as a coach. The key is to be able to enter into this state of attention without looking as if you're in a trance! This can take a little practice.

Thoughts

The image of your client that you hold inside your mind is one of the most important parts of the coaching state. We have a saying in HNLP that another person can never be better in your presence than the image you hold of him or her.

It is therefore very important that you hold an image of your client as a totally resourceful and powerful being—as someone who has already begun to make the changes he or she wants.

Preframing the BEAT System

Before you do any NLP pattern with a coaching client, it's always good to lay down appropriate preframes for the client to follow. The BEAT System is no exception. In this section, we will discuss some standard preframes that you might want to use before you begin the BEAT with your coaching client.

One useful preframe is the compliance preframe. This preframe is simply designed to ensure that your coaching client will go along with your suggestions and instructions.

The easiest way of building a compliance preframe is to ask your client to follow a number of noncontroversial suggestions before you move into doing any NLP pattern. (For this example, we will be using the pronoun *she* throughout.) For example, you may ask your client to sit in a particular chair, put her feet flat on the floor, fill out the intake form, relax her breathing, or follow similar instructions that she is unlikely to question.

Once your client has begun to follow your instructions in the simple matters, she is likely to continue following your instructions when you get to the more unusual steps of the BEAT System.

Another aspect of compliance is rapport. As long as your client likes and respects you, she is much more likely to go along with your instructions. Creating and maintaining the "coaching bubble" will likely generate an excellent state of rapport.

Not only do you want your coaching client to go along with your suggestions, but to do so with the expectation that they will lead to a positive change in her life. There are number of ways to do this, for example:

- You can explain the neuroscience behind the BEAT. Neuroscience provides one of the most powerful sets of metaphors you can use to convince your client of the power of a particular technique.
- You can explain how the BEAT System has transformed the lives of other clients (or even how it has transformed your life).
- You can use simple embedded commands. Perhaps you want to say, "I'm going to teach you a simple technique that *you can take away with you and use* to *easily change any negative state* and *step into a peak performance state* at will."

Choosing a Context

Before you begin teaching the BEAT System to your coaching client, you and she need to select a specific time and place in which she will use it. The more specific you can be, the better. When will she use it—what day and time? Where will she be? What is she seeing and hearing there? Who else is there with her?

The more narrowly you focus this choice of context, the better. We know this sounds counterintuitive—after all, wouldn't it be better to have her apply the BEAT in many contexts? The answer, of course, is yes; however, she has to apply it first in one specific place. Once you've taught her the BEAT System and she has mentally rehearsed using it in that specific context, it is easy enough to lead her to rehearse the BEAT in another context, and then another context, and so on. This will allow her unconscious mind to easily generalize the BEAT System across many contexts.

Choosing an Outcome

Once your client has selected the context in which she wants to use the BEAT, you should lead her to choose an outcome that is appropriate for that context. This should include:

- What does she want to achieve in the context?
- How will she know she has achieved this? She should be able to visualize what she will be seeing and hearing when she has achieved the outcome. This visualization will become the basis of her thoughts ("T") within the BEAT.
- How will the other people in the context be behaving toward her?
- How is she using her body to achieve this outcome? For example, if she is in a business meeting sitting around the table with her colleagues, *how* will she be sitting? What will her posture and breathing be like? This will become the basis of her body and breathing ("B") within the BEAT.
- What emotional state will be most useful to her in achieving this outcome? This will become the basis of her emotional state ("E") within the BEAT.
- What should she be directing her attention toward in order to achieve this outcome? Should her attention be focused, or should she be using peripheral vision? This will be the basis of her attention ("A")

within the BEAT.

You now have the context in which your client wants to change, and you know what the outcome is. All that remains is to directionalize that unconscious change toward that outcome within that specific context.

Before we move on to teaching her the BEAT System, it is a good idea to get all these ducks in a row!

In particular, you should make sure your client is familiar with peripheral vision. Whether or not she is, you should lead her through the experience of going into peripheral vision several times and anchoring it as discussed previously.

You also need to make sure she is comfortable getting in touch with the emotions inside her body. Some people are unfamiliar with scanning their own body for feelings, particularly emotional feelings. Again, we refer you to the earlier chapter on the emotional step of the BEAT System for details on how to do this.

Finally, you need to make sure that your coaching client is comfortable with visualization—in particular, visualizing her outcome. You should spend enough time building this visualization up and using submodalities (size, brightness, location, and so on) to make it more compelling. You should also make sure that the "title" of the movie is positive and compelling.

Okay, now you are ready to move into the BEAT System itself.

The Physiology of Excellence

Leading your client to step into a positive physiology is probably the most important part of teaching her the

BEAT. If you are able to lead her into a positive physiology, she will more than likely automatically feel a positive emotional state. Remember, our physiology and our emotional state are linked together. Step into a positive physiology, and it's very difficult to maintain a negative state.

Therefore, when you are teaching her the first step of the BEAT, you might say something like:

> *I'd like you to imagine that standing in front of you is your ideal self. This is the "you" who can easily achieve your outcome, who already has that sense of confidence. Make that picture big and bright, and when you see it very clearly in front of you, step forward into it...*

As you say this, you are watching your client to see a change in her physiology. You do not want her physiology to change when she steps forward into the picture—you want her physiology to change *before* she takes that step forward. This change in physiology will then be unconscious for your client. It will be a reflection of the change in her inner state.

When you see the change in her physiology, you can invite her to step forward into the image of her ideal self and then squeeze her thumb and forefinger together, "B." Remember, get the change in physiology first, then step forward, and then anchor. It is much, much easier if you do it this way because her internal state will automatically be positive.

Repeat this first step, if necessary, until you see that automatic physiological shift each time she steps forward into her ideal self.

Emotions

Assuming you have done the first step of the BEAT in the way suggested above, the second step is simple. You will simply invite your client to:

Go inside and notice how you're feeling...

If you have achieved the unconscious physiological shift, she will go inside and—surprise, surprise—find that she is feeling very good indeed.

Of course, you may need to build up this internal emotional state using kinesthetic submodalities. For example, you may want to invite her to:

Spin that feeling faster. Spread it through every cell, every muscle, every fiber of your body. Intensify the color and add sparkles...

Emotional Coaching

Of course, it's possible that when you ask your client to go inside and notice how she feels, she will report a negative feeling.

The first response might be to consider whether she really had an unconscious physiological shift in step one. If not, you might want to go back and repeat step one.

Alternatively, it might be that she has some negative block about the context that is sufficiently strong to dampen the effects of the BEAT. For example, if she has a strong fear of speaking in public based upon her beliefs about herself or her self-identity as a "failure," simply installing the BEAT may not be sufficient to overcome this.

Remember, the BEAT essentially addresses the bottom

four Sephirot of the Tree of Life. If she holds negative beliefs about herself or a negative self-identity, these beliefs and this identity represent higher-level Sephirot on the Tree of Life (see our book *Tree of Life Coaching* for further clarification).

If this is the case, it may be necessary to address these issues first. You could do this using any standard NLP, coaching, or hypnosis technique, such as the NLP belief change, reframing, hypnotic ego boosting, and so on.

Of course, you can also use the 90-second rule. You can ask your client to get in touch with the location, size, and shape of a negative feeling. Holding her attention on that feeling within the body, you can invite her to notice how the size, shape, and location change over time. You'll almost always find that it dissipates as long as you are able to keep her attention within the body so she does not "throw logs on the fire" of the negative emotion.

Another way of doing this that can work well with clients who have a problem keeping their attention on the feeling within the body (typically clients who have a lot of self-talk) is to use distraction. Once your client has told you that she is feeling the negative emotion and has told you where in her body she feels it, you might say something like:

That reminds me of a story...

You can then launch into a metaphor that has absolutely nothing to do with what she just said. As she tries to make sense of your metaphor, her attention will automatically move off her negative feeling, allowing it the 90 seconds it needs to dissipate. When you see the shift in her physiology that lets you know her negative feeling has changed, you can simply ask her:

How you feeling now? ... Really? You mean that negative

feeling has gone away? Remind me how you want to feel instead… And when you're feeling that now, where do you feel it within your body?

Either way, once the negative emotion has died away, you can replace it with a positive emotion by asking:

What's important to you about making this change? [Suppose she says, "It will give me freedom."] *And when you are being free now, where do you feel it in your body?*

The answer to this question is the feeling that should be attached to the "E" of the BEAT.

When the client is in a positive emotional state, you can get her to anchor it by stepping forward into the second position and squeezing her thumb and middle finger together.

Awareness

It is now time to move on to the next step of the BEAT—awareness. If you're using peripheral vision, this will be easy because you have already taught it to her and installed it before you even began the BEAT.

Simply invite her to step forward into third position, fire off the anchors for peripheral vision, and when you see her going to the peripheral vision states, invite her to squeeze her thumb and ring finger together.

You now have the first three steps of the BEAT installed.

Installing New Thoughts

Now it is time to move on to the final step of the BEAT—"T" or thoughts.

Because you've spent some time exploring the client's outcome and making sure she has a strong visual representation of this outcome with powerful and compelling submodalities and a positive title, this final step is also easy.

Simply invite her to step forward and make the picture of her outcome within her mind's eye. She should see what she will be seeing and hear what she will be hearing,

She might also want to use her inner dialogue to repeat the title of this movie.

Now that you have installed each step of the BEAT, it's time for you to begin conditioning it. The only way to do this is through repetition.

So, get the client to step back to the start of the chain, before she took the first step, and once more,

> *See the ideal "you," step forward into that, and squeeze your thumb and forefinger together…*
>
> *Step forward again and notice how good you feel as you squeeze your thumb and middle finger together…*
>
> *Step forward and go into peripheral vision as you squeeze your thumb and ring finger together…*
>
> *And as you take that last step forward, make a movie in your mind of your outcome, give it a great title, and squeeze your thumb and little finger together.*

Future Pacing

All that remains is to have your client mentally rehearse using the BEAT System in the specific context she has chosen. Get her to imagine being in that context and firing off the four anchors, either by taking the four steps and/or by squeezing her thumb and fingers together one after another.

Once you have done this, if you wish, you can get her to select another context and repeat the BEAT in that new context.

Chapter 15: The Hypnotic BEAT

In this chapter, we will discuss ways that you can use the BEAT in your hypnosis practice, if you are a hypnotist.

Of course, if you are the sort of hypnotist who blends traditional hypnosis with NLP and other modalities, you can simply use the coaching BEAT described in Chapter 14.

Direct Suggestion

If you are more of a classical hypnotist who believes in dropping your client into a closed-eye trance and giving him or her direct suggestions, what should you do? In actuality, the BEAT is a wonderful system to have in your tool kit for direct suggestions because it offers multiple ways to offer the same related suggestions.

Suppose your client wishes to be more creative while writing in his or her office. Traditionally you might have suggested something like:

- *You are a creative person...*

By keeping the BEAT in mind, you can easily and naturally create many more suggestions based on creative physiology, creative emotional states, creative sensory awareness, and creative thoughts, all within the context in which the client wants that creativity.

You can then anchor the various pieces of the creative BEAT you just installed to contextual anchors within that so that the BEAT will fire off automatically when the client steps into that context.

So you might say something like:

> *You are a creative person so that...*
>
> *... you literally feel your body beginning to open up to new possibilities, as you...*
>
> *... feel that rush of creative energy begin to flow through you, while...*
>
> *... you begin to notice things that you've never seen before, experiencing the world in a new way as...*
>
> *... new and original thoughts begin to appear in your mind...*
>
> *... each and every time you sit down in your office to write, so that seeing your computer screen...*
>
> *... you feel your body becoming more open to creativity, which means that you can feel even more...*

... creative energy flowing through you, since...

... you see the world in a new way, leading to...

... even more creative thoughts...

and so on.

Indirect Suggestion

For those hypnotists with a more Ericksonian approach who utilize indirect suggestion, you could start your session with something like:

> *You know how some people just seem to <u>be more creative</u>, there's something about the way they <u>sit creatively</u>, their creative posture* [shifting posture to be more upright] *that lets <u>you know creative things are going on within you</u>, <u>sense it. Now</u>...*
>
> *... what you feel inside, when <u>you are your most creative</u> self, is unique to each individual. Some people may <u>feel a surge of energy</u> or perhaps <u>feel a tingling</u> that lets you know great <u>new ideas are on your way</u>... to becoming even more creative*
>
> *because when <u>you feel creative</u>, you begin to <u>see the world in a new way</u>, new possibilities open up...*
> *... ideas begin to link up inside your mind in new ways...*

Chapter 16: The Recovery BEAT

In this chapter, we will be discussing an application of the BEAT that you can use when things go wrong. We like to call this the Recovery BEAT because it allows you to recover your composure under even the most difficult circumstances.

The Recovery BEAT is based on a pattern developed by our good friend and teacher John Overdurf. Each step of the Recovery BEAT is designed, using principles of neuroscience and research, to take you out of a "fight, flight or freeze" mode and into a place where you can regain control of yourself and the situation around you.

You'll know it's time to use the Recovery BEAT when you notice that your physiology has shifted to a less than resourceful posture. Or if you begin to feel nervous, stressed, or another similarly un-resourceful state. Or if you find that your attention is focused on something that is not important, or useful, or helpful. Or if your brain starts to run negative thoughts or self-talk. No matter what the cause, the result of falling out of your peak state is that your emotions shift into a state that is not resourceful or useful. This negative state begins to change your physiology, your sensory awareness, and your thoughts, creating a spiral of negativity.

The best way to teach you this version of the BEAT is to walk through each of the steps individually. Because this pattern is based on a negative shift in your emotional state, and because your emotional state is a piece of your experience that is most difficult to *consciously* control, we are going to leave the emotional piece until last.

Step 1: Body

The first step of the Recovery BEAT uses a simple physiological trick that will take you immediately out of a "fight, flight or freeze" response.

This simply involves relaxing and dropping your jaw. Try it now: drop your jaw so that your teeth are slightly separated. Relax your jaw so that your lower jaw can easily move from side to side. You might even want to use your hands to gently move your lower jaw from side to side to get used to this sense of relaxation.

There are several reasons that this jaw dropping is so effective. The first reason is physiological: dropping your jaw stimulates your vagus nerve, which moves you away from a "fight, flight or freeze" response and toward a "rest and digest" state of relaxation.

The second reason is evolutionary. The jaw is one of the weakest parts of the body and could easily be broken if, for example, you got into a fight. In nature, a broken jaw could be very serious because it could prevent you from eating. Therefore, there is a very strong evolutionary driver that causes you to "clench" your jaw when you're angry or when your body otherwise perceives danger. Relaxing your jaw sends exactly the opposite message to your body—that the danger is over and you are safe.

At the same time, as you relax and drop your jaw, you can take a deep breath in, followed by a long breath out. Once again, this control of your breathing overrides the rapid breathing you are likely to experience when you are afraid and sends a signal to your physiology that you are safe.

Step 2: Emotions

As we said above, you're only likely to need a recovery strategy if something triggers you to go into a negative state.

Because your emotional state is the most difficult of the elements of the BEAT to control, we will leave it till last.

Step 3: Awareness

As we've noted before, foveal vision is associated with the approach of danger. When we feel we are in danger, we tend to put all our focused attention on whatever we perceive the source of that danger to be.

In contrast, when you go into peripheral vision, you send a strong physiological signal to your brain and body that there is no danger.

Therefore, the third step of the Recovery BEAT is simply to go into peripheral vision. Again, you can practice this by holding your hands up in front of you so you can see the backs of your hands. Gently wave your fingers as you separate your hands. Move your hands apart, continuing to gaze at a point directly in front of you halfway between your two hands. Separate your hands until they "disappear" and you can no longer see the movement of your fingers in your peripheral vision.

Practice this until you can enter peripheral vision easily.

Step 4: Thoughts

Research shows that when you imagine moving forward, you are more likely to experience positive feelings than if you imagine being still (with things moving toward you) or imagine moving backward.

This is probably due to the "fight, flight, or freeze" response. We freeze or go backward in response to danger. Moving forward sends a strong message to your unconscious mind that you are in control.

Therefore, the fourth step of the Recovery BEAT is to imagine moving forward. You can do this in any way that makes sense to you based on the context. One simple method you might like to try is to imagine you are moving forward through the air, possibly soaring like a bird (obviously, don't try this technique if you have a fear of heights!).

So let's summarize where we are:
- B: Drop and loosen your jaw, breathing in deeply and breathing out slowly.
- E: (still to come)
- A: Go to peripheral vision.
- T: Imagine moving forward toward your goal.

Once you have been through the Recovery BEAT, check in with your feelings once more. Chances are that the previous three steps will have brought you to a state of calm and relaxation.

If you're still feeling nervous, fearful, or otherwise in a negative state, run through the Recovery BEAT again.

Once your emotions have calmed down, it's time to return to the second step of the Recovery BEAT. Ask yourself what is important to you about being here, at this time and in this place, doing what you're doing right now. What does this do for you? What is important about it—what is the value attached to it?

Now ask yourself how you are being as a person when you are already living this value. And notice where in your body you feel that.

Using the Recovery BEAT in Practice

Perhaps you have a tendency, when you go into a negative state, to either freeze up or begin reacting without proper thought. I know I do—it's as if time either stops or speeds up. Either I can't say anything at all, or I have to say everything at once! In fact, people who take a minute or two to think before reacting, particularly when they are under pressure, come across as being much more in control. If you need an opportunity to seize the minute that you need, simply ask for it: "Let me think about that for a moment."

This will make you appear to be both wise and in control. It will also provide you with the time you need to recover by:

- Dropping your jaw and taking a breath, "B"
- Going into peripheral vision, "A"
- Imagining moving forward, "T"
- And finally, asking yourself what's important about being in this time and place, "E"

Now you're ready to step back into your ideal self and carry on being the best you can be!

Chapter 17: The BEAT for Meditation

In this chapter, we will describe a version of the BEAT that can be used for meditation, particularly for walking meditation.

What Is Walking Meditation?

In walking meditation, you simply walk, preferably in nature, although performing walking meditation when traversing the busy sidewalks of New York is an experience unto itself.

While you are walking, you focus your mind on your steps. Thich Nhat Hahn, the Buddhist monk, makes the following suggestion for walking meditation:

> *Try visualizing a lotus flower opening as your feet touch the ground like a newborn Buddha.*

You'll notice that Thich Nhat Hahn is talking about visualization—one type of "thought" as we have defined that word. You do not necessarily need to clear your mind to engage in walking meditation; instead, you can focus the mind on one thought as long as you gently bring your mind back to this thought whenever it strays.

Thich Nhat Hahn also suggests the use of a mantra,

"I am home."

This short phrase can be repeated as your inner dialogue as you walk. You might want to break the mantra into two parts, perhaps saying, "I am" as your left foot touches the ground, and "home" as your right foot touches the ground. Alternatively, you might want to repeat each part on alternate out-breaths.

Using the BEAT for Walking Meditation

From the above description, you can see that we already have two elements of the BEAT System in the traditional walking meditation. We have the body taking gentle steps, and we have the thoughts visualizing a lotus flower opening before you and the inner voice repeating the mantra "I am... home."

To complete the BEAT for walking meditation, you simply have to check in and adjust your emotional state and be aware of your own awareness. Let's take awareness first.

Awareness in Walking Meditation

In an earlier chapter, we described how to go into peripheral vision and how to condition the state of peripheral vision so it becomes natural. Peripheral vision is an excellent way to perceive the world when you are practicing walking meditation. If you are walking in nature, using peripheral vision allows you to more fully appreciate the beauty of the world around you.

If you're walking in the busy streets of a city, peripheral vision allows you to be aware of the people, bicycles, and cars around you, how they are moving relative to your path, how fast they are going, and so on. Being in peripheral vision allows you to more easily navigate crowded areas without bumping into people. In fact, when you're walking and using peripheral vision, you will be amazed at how space simply seems to open up in front of you.

Emotions in Walking Meditation

All that's left is for you to get in touch with your emotional state. Before you do this, there is a very important question for you to ask yourself: "*Why* am I engaging in walking meditation? What is important about it to me?"

For example, you may practice walking meditation because you want to achieve a state of daily peace and calm. The question then becomes how you feel inside your body when you are in a state of peace and calm. This is the feeling you want to cultivate as you walk. How do you cultivate this feeling? Simply by asking yourself the question: "How do I feel when I'm in a state of peace and calm?" Asking yourself this question automatically sends a signal to the mind-body to find the state of peace and calm.

Summary of the System

We now have the four elements of the BEAT for walking meditation.

Firstly, decide when and where you want to practice walking meditation. Of course, "now" is always a good time, and "here" is always a good place.

Once you are ready to begin, imagine that your spine is suspended from a silver cord attached to the sky. Feel your feet resting on the floor and the earth supporting your weight. Slowly and gently step forward by shifting all your weight to your supporting foot, freeing your stepping foot. Feel your stepping foot as it comes to rest on the ground. As you do so, squeeze your thumb and forefinger together. This is the first step of the BEAT.

Now take your second step forward—one small step—and feel your foot as it comes to rest gently on the ground. As it does, check inside and notice how you feel. If you feel peace and calm, all is well and good.

If you don't feel peace and calm, for example, if you feel anxious or impatient or stressed, simply remember the 90-second rule and the self-coaching pattern. Notice where in your body you feel that negative emotion and notice the size and shape of the feeling and whether it has a color, temperature, or texture. Now simply wait, keeping your attention on that feeling until it dissipates.

As the feeling dissipates, simply ask yourself how you would be feeling if you were feeling peace and calm right now. Notice where in your body you are feeling that now. Once you're feeling your state of peace and calm, squeeze your thumb and middle finger together. You have completed the second step of the BEAT.

If you check in with your feelings and they are positive, even if they are not the peace and calm you were expecting, I would suggest that you feel calm and peaceful about this and can move onto the next step.

Once you have completed the second step, it's time to take your third step forward. Take that step now and feel your foot come to rest on the ground. As you take this third step, allow yourself to go into peripheral vision and peripheral hearing. Enjoy the world around you, and as you do so, squeeze your thumb and ring finger together. You have completed the third step of the BEAT.

Take your fourth step forward, and as your foot descends to the ground, visualize a lotus flower opening beneath it, and feel your foot gently touch the lotus flower. Using your inner voice, say, "I am." Squeeze your thumb and pinky together. This is the fourth step of the BEAT.
Now we are ready to roll.

Take another step forward, visualizing a lotus flower opening as your foot gently touches the ground and your inner voice says, "... home" and your eyes gently observe the world around you from peripheral vision.
You might want to put a little more attention on the feeling of your foot touching the ground as you squeeze your thumb and forefinger together.

Step forward again, your foot gently coming to rest on the lotus flower, listening to the world with peripheral hearing, "I am," and check in with your emotional state. Are you feeling peace and calm?

Continue in this way. After a few steps, we guarantee that you will be in a state of deep meditation!

The Variations

There are many variations of the BEAT for meditation, whether walking, sitting, or otherwise.

For example, when completing the first step of the BEAT, rather than putting your attention entirely on your foot touching the floor, you might instead want to put your attention on your breath. Breathing from your belly, push your belly out as you breathe in by pushing your diaphragm down. As you breathe out, allow your diaphragm to move up, and your belly will naturally move in. If you allow your out-breath to be twice as long as your in-breath, you will begin to stimulate your parasympathetic ("rest and digest") nervous system.

If you find the idea of visualizing a lotus flower opening under each step a little hokey, you might instead visualize a ball of light floating above your head. Perhaps that is hokey as well, but there is a good reason for it, which we are about to explain.

When you visualize a ball of light above your head, it tends to elongate your spine, making your posture more upright and allowing you to walk more freely.

We generally suggest that you visualize an orange ball of light simply because for many people, the color orange is associated with creativity. Research demonstrates that walking also aids creativity, so if you engage in regular walking meditation, you may find yourself being more creative than you ever believed possible!

Chapter 18: The Social BEAT

In this chapter, we will talk about using the BEAT in social situations. Perhaps you are going on a date or simply attending a party. You're not looking for "peak performance," or to amaze your business clients with your presentation skills, or to shoot your best ever round of golf—you just want to have fun.

If so, this is the BEAT System for you!

For many people, being in a social situation is fully as stressful as going on a sales call. You would think it would be easy to relax socially, but you find yourself worrying about how to introduce yourself to the attractive woman or man you see at the party, or how to keep the conversation going on a second date now that you've already asked all the obvious questions.

If so, this is the BEAT System for you!

Alternatively, you may be at a business meet and greet. You are faced with a roomful of strangers who are all clearly more interesting, important, and socially adept than you are. You feel like standing in the corner and hoping that nobody notices you.

If so, this is the BEAT System for you!

Let's dive right in and take each of the four steps of the BEAT System one by one.

Step 1: Body and Breathing

In every case, it goes without saying that preparing your body for the BEAT begins before you ever step into the situation. This rule goes doubly for the social BEAT. You will definitely want to make sure that you are well groomed and dressed to impress. Take a look in the mirror before you step out of your apartment. If you're looking smoking hot, it's time to go!

Within a social situation, your physiology immediately sends many important messages to the other people in the room. In a business situation, your colleagues or clients *have* to speak to you and listen to you. If you are in a sports competition, your opponent *has* to pay attention to you. But when you're in a social situation, your body language will determine how approachable you appear and therefore how many times you are approached as well as the reaction you get when you approach someone else.

The next time you're in a social situation, look around at the other people and notice who seems most approachable. (For this example, we will be using the pronoun *he* throughout.) Now ask yourself the question, "Why does he appear approachable? What is it about that person that makes him appear approachable?"

If you do this a few times, you'll find some common threads. For example, it's very likely that he will be smiling. He will probably be making a lot of eye contact with the people around him, and when he does, he will look interested and curious. He may be nodding his head as people speak, or he may be tilting his head to one side to let the other people know he is interested. He will probably be using open body language, inviting people into his space by showing open palm gestures, and keeping his arms at his sides or at least not held in front of him.

If you're not naturally gregarious, it may be surprising to discover that the social butterfly you admire so much is simply using a few body-language tools to send out a powerful message of approachability.

Once you have identified the "physiology of social excellence," imagine your ideal social self standing in front of you using this type of body language. When you're ready, you can step into that ideal "you" and take on that physiology.

In our experience, some of our clients have a real problem with this step. They literally "can't see" themselves acting socially, particularly if they suffer from shyness or some other type of social anxiety. If this is the case for you, you may want to imagine somebody else standing in front of you—somebody whom you see as being more socially adept.

Whichever way you choose, practice stepping into this new social "you," and as you step forward, fire your kinesthetic anchor. As always, but particularly in this case, if you have squeezed your thumb and forefinger together to anchor this state, you should do so very subtly. After all, if you walk around the party tapping your fingers together, it could send an altogether different impression!

They say there are two types of people in the world—extroverts and introverts. Whether you are an extrovert or an introvert has nothing to do with how socially adept you are; instead, it has to do with how you "recharge your batteries."

You see, extroverts recharge their batteries by being in social situations. An extrovert could go to a party on Friday night feeling exhausted after a week's work and leave the party feeling totally energized. In contrast, introverts recharge their batteries by spending time by themselves or maybe with a couple of close friends. If an introvert goes to a party, he or she may leave feeling exhausted because of having used so much energy on social interaction.

If you're going to be socially adept, you really have to understand what sort of person you are. Are you an introvert or an extrovert? If you're an extrovert, you will probably find it relatively easy to maintain an open and positive emotional state at the party.

However, if you are an introvert, you need to be prepared to put some energy into your social interactions! One of the easiest ways of creating and maintaining the emotional state you need in order to become a true social butterfly is to think in terms of curiosity. If you become intensely curious about the person you're speaking to, you will have fun, and the other person will feel valued. Stepping into a state of curiosity generates the brain chemical dopamine, which is part of the brain's reward circuit. Dopamine makes you feel good as you learn. It's sort of the brain's way of bribing you to do your homework!

Here's one way of generating the curiosity you will need in order to generate the necessary dopamine, have fun, and make this whole process enjoyable. All you have to do is realize that every single person on the face of the earth has at least one thing that makes him or her truly fascinating. I remember being among a group of people at a business meet and greet at which I asked one young lady what the most fascinating thing about her was. She blushed slightly as she admitted there was absolutely nothing about her that was interesting, but when I pressed a little further, she admitted that she enjoyed making sourdough bread. It took only another question or two before she was joyfully explaining to the group the finer points of making the dough and how the best yeasts were kept for decades or even centuries, being fed and kept alive by their owners. She explained why the sourdough on the West Coast was much better than the sourdough on the East Coast because of the atmospheric conditions. The group was enthralled, not so much by the topic, perhaps, but by the passion and energy she brought to the conversation. Not only did they leave knowing more about sourdough bread than they ever thought possible, but she left an indelible impression on the group as the "sourdough lady."

Every single person you meet has his or her own story, his or her own "sourdough." For some people it will be music, for other people it will be collecting candy wrappers. For some people it will be skydiving, and for others it will be astronomy. If you remain curious enough to get people talking about something they love, you will find it fascinating, and they will believe you to be the best listener they have ever met!

Remember as well that the power of the BEAT System lies in the fact that each piece of the BEAT supports and amplifies the other pieces. If you adopt the physiology of curiosity—for example, by tilting your head to one side, slightly widening your eyes, nodding your head as the other person speaks, smiling, and so on—you will begin to *feel* more curious. And the opposite is also true: as you begin to feel more curious, your physiology will naturally take on the expressions of curiosity, and your conversational partner will open up more. In this case, one plus one does not equal two—it equals three.

Step 3: Awareness

They say that the eyes are the windows to the soul. When you look at the structure of the eye, you will see that it is designed for social interaction. Think about it—your eye is a thing of beauty: a small black pupil surrounded by a beautifully colored and patterned iris, which in turn is surrounded by a milky white. Eyes are particularly beautiful and deserve to be admired.

The way the eye is structured, with the colored iris surrounded by the white, it is designed to show exactly in which direction the eye is pointing, which is to say, exactly who is looking at you.

The Eyes Show Who Is Attracted to You

In a psychological research study, participants were asked to rate the attractiveness of various photos of members of the opposite sex. Having ranked the photos according to attractiveness, the participants were asked why they found certain people more attractive, and they came up with reasons such as "Oh, she looks nice" or "He looks athletic" or whatever they found attractive. In fact, the researchers had Photo-shopped the pictures to make the pupils of the eyes larger or smaller in some photographs. In general, the participants rated someone as more attractive based on whether the pupils of their eyes appeared larger, even though the participants were not aware of this consciously. When we find somebody attractive, the pupils of our eyes actually expand to let in more light, as if we can't see enough of the other person. And this pupil expansion sends a powerful unconscious signal to the other person to communicate that we find him or her attractive.

We Are Designed to See People Blush

The insides of our eyes are also designed for social interaction. The eye is particularly sensitive to a certain wavelength of light that corresponds precisely to the color of human blood underneath the skin. We are engineered to see people blush, and blushing is frequently a sign of attraction, too.

Social Interaction and Eye Movement

When you are engaged in a social conversation with somebody, the movement of your eyes as you look at him or her tells that person unconsciously what sort of conversation it is. For example, if you are deeply attracted to a woman, you might stare into her eyes; however, if you have only just met her, staring into her eyes for more than a few seconds may be socially inappropriate.

Instead, social eye contact generally consists of looking at each of her eyes in turn as well as her mouth, so your eyes will move around the triangle that is formed by her two eyes and mouth. The reason we tell you this is that when we suggest you look at the person you're talking to, we don't want you to end up staring at him or her!

For social awareness, we are going to suggest a technique similar to the one discussed in the coaching BEAT. Begin by going into peripheral vision by holding your hands out in front of you at arm's length so you are looking at the backs of your hands with your fingers pointing vertically upward (obviously, this is for you to practice when you are alone—don't do this at the party or on a date!). Now begin by wiggling your fingers as you slowly move your hands out to the sides at shoulder height. As usual, your hands will seem to reach a point where they disappear from view as they move out of your zone of peripheral vision.

Now begin to move them back in toward the center. As they move in, allow your attention to rest in the space in between your left and right hands. This means that you are paying attention to the space between your hands, but NOT the space outside your hands. As your hands move in, the zone of your attention becomes narrower, and if you move your hands back out again, your zone of attention becomes wider.

Practice this until you can make your zone of attention as wide or as narrow as you want without using your hands.

Now you're ready for the social gaze.

Find a partner to practice with. If you don't have a partner, you can look at yourself in a mirror or go down to your local coffee shop and have a chat with somebody. As you talk to that person, place your awareness on the area immediately surrounding him or her, as if you are putting a caring "bubble" of attention around the person.

This is the part where it is important for you to move your eyes around in the triangle framed by the person's two eyes and mouth. If you don't do this, you may end up staring at him or her like a zombie and making him or her feel uncomfortable! Once you have mastered this method of making a visual connection with another person, you can very quickly and easily make the person feel listened to and cared for.

Another benefit of looking at someone in this way is that you will immediately begin to notice the gestures that the person uses. This will allow you to build rapport with him or her by repeating back some of these gestures in a respectful and subtle way (something called mirroring and matching).

Now it's time to begin to add in a certain type of listening. Just as you wrapped your visual attention around the person, you can also begin to wrap your auditory attention around him or her. This involves not just listening to the words the person uses, but also listening carefully for changes in his or her tonality.

Don't worry about what these changes in tonality mean. The simple act of listening carefully and respectfully to the person means that you are beginning to tap into a whole band of information that is normally only tracked by your unconscious mind. When you do this for a while, you will begin to get flashes of insight about that person. You may not know where these insights come from consciously, because they are simply your mind beginning to pick up on the million subtle clues that each of us gives out as part of our communication.

Step 4: Thoughts

There is an old video of Dr. Richard Bandler, cofounder of NLP, working with a client who suffers from shyness. Bandler is asking the client about his experience when he is in a social situation where he wants to speak to a woman. Bandler repeatedly asks him if he is seeing a picture inside his mind, and the client repeatedly says no.

Because Bandler is tracking the client's eye movements— movements that indicate what sort of mental processes the client is using—Bandler finally loses his patience and says something like, "I can see you're making pictures inside your mind. What are they?" The client is startled for a moment and then says, "Oh yes, I can see a picture of her face as she sneers at me!"

We all have thoughts that move through our minds all the time, telling us how to act. Very often, we are not even aware of these thoughts—they form a sort of mental wallpaper or background. So, if you want to have fun at the party, it's a pretty good idea to make this mental wallpaper bright and cheery.

Bandler tells his client to change the picture from the woman sneering at him to one of her smiling at him. This simple change, together with a few other changes (in NLP, we call this a strategy installation), are enough to turn the client from a shy wallflower to a gregarious and outgoing party animal.

So the final step of the social BEAT is to create a picture in your mind of people smiling.

Try it now. Within your mind's eye, begin to generate a series of pictures of people smiling. Notice what happens to your own face: you are likely to find yourself smiling as well. This is a natural human reaction; when somebody smiles at you, you will likely smile back. When you make pictures inside your head of people smiling, you are likely to start smiling as well, and when you start smiling, guess what happens? That's right! People start smiling back at you! You have created reality using the power of your imagination! Isn't that cool?

And while you're at it, you might as well hear them speaking to you in warm, honeyed tones.

So, here we go with the social BEAT:

Imagine you are in a specific social situation. Where are you? When is this? Who else is there? Be specific.

Step 1: See your ideal social self in front of you (use another person, if necessary). Notice how that ideal social "you" is standing and notice his or her gestures and facial expression. Make the picture big and bright, and when you're ready, step into your best social self. Anchor this physiology by squeezing your thumb and forefinger together, "B."

Step 2: Open up to an intense sense of curiosity about the people and the world around you. Where do you feel that sense of curiosity? Move that feeling through each cell of your body. Anchor this feeling of curiosity by squeezing your thumb and middle finger together, "E."

Step 3: Go into peripheral vision, and then within your field of vision, wrap your attention around the person in front of you. Make sure to move your eyes within the social triangle defined by the person's two eyes and mouth. Listen to his or her tonality. Anchor this sensory awareness by squeezing your thumb and ring finger together, "A."

Step 4: Make a picture within your mind's eye of the person smiling at you and nodding. Imagine that he or she is speaking to you in a warm tone of voice. Anchor these thoughts by squeezing your thumb and pinky together, "T."

Run through this sequence as many times as it takes to install it.

Now think of another social situation and repeat the above steps.

The next time you're going to a social interaction, run through these steps, imagining that situation.

Finally, attach that first picture of your ideal social self to something you will actually see in that context using the Swish BEAT pattern described in Chapter 9.

Chapter 19: The Business BEAT

In this chapter, we will discuss various ways you can use the BEAT System in business. After all, it is probably more important to have state control in the business environment than anywhere else. For example, if you are practicing your favorite sport, you need to be in the performance states for that sport, whether that state is focused concentration or unbridled aggression or whatever.

In business, things are a little bit different, as you will need to move from one state to another many times during the course of your typical business day. You might need to be inspirational when you address your colleagues in the weekly team meeting, then step into a state of logical analytical focus when you read through a report, then step into a state of conspiratorial friendliness when you take your mentee to lunch, and then step into a state of gregariousness when you take your client out to dinner.

If you are not able to change your state very easily and quickly, you may get a bad reputation. For example, a trial lawyer who only has access to his confrontational state that he uses in court may get a reputation as a difficult boss. On the other hand, a boss who is wonderful at connecting and building bonds with his staff may get a reputation as lacking the "killer instinct" when negotiating a contract. The fact is that different contexts require different states. The BEAT System is ideal for switching from one state to another at will.

Overview of the BEAT System for Business

There is nothing different about using the BEAT in business compared to any other context. You can use spatial anchors by using the last four footsteps as you walk into a room or onto a podium, if you are giving a speech.

Alternatively, you can use the kinesthetic anchors by pressing the thumb together with each of the fingertips in turn, for example, if you are sitting down and want to do the BEAT surreptitiously.

To set up and condition the BEAT, you have to decide on your ideal physiology, emotional state, focus and awareness of the world, and thoughts. This is the fun part because each of those peak states you want to achieve will have different physiologies, emotional states, awareness, and thoughts associated with them.

Let's go back to our example of the typical business day. Our intrepid businesswoman (lets call her Mary) has four things on her agenda:
1. Inspiring the weekly team meeting
2. Reviewing a report
3. Taking her mentee to lunch
4. Taking her client to dinner

We will take each section in turn and include a brief exercise for you to practice these skills.

Inspiring Her Team

What is the physiology of inspiration? It is likely to involve wide gestures, perhaps Mary gestures with her hands held out at shoulder height. Her chin might be tilted upward a little, as if she were gazing into the future.

What about Mary's emotional state? Perhaps she feels a sense of passion and yearning for the future that is almost within reach.

Her vision might be on the possible future she sees. At the same time, Mary will be aware of the effect that her words have on her audience through her peripheral vision, while she makes individual eye contact with each member of the group to draw them into the passion she feels for this vision.

And Mary's thoughts need to be congruent with all this. Within her mind's eye, she needs to see that future playing on the movie screen of her mind. And the title of the movie needs to be something like, "We can do this—we're almost there!"

Exercise

One of the best ways of building the elements of this state—including the physiology, the emotional states, the sensory awareness, and the thoughts—is to choose a model whom you admire in that situation. We will use the pronoun *he* for all these exercises. Who do you know who is totally inspirational? What is that ideal person like when he is speaking? What are his gestures like? Is he paying attention to one tiny detail or to the whole? What pictures do you imagine he is making in his mind? Remember, these pictures will reveal themselves in the words the model uses.

Reviewing the Report

Let's shift now to consider the optimal state for Mary while reviewing a report.

Perhaps her physiology is sitting upright at her desk.

Is her emotional state one of patient determination? Or perhaps creativity?

Mary might be in foveal vision as she focuses on each word of the report. Maybe she turns her head away and gazes into the distance in peripheral vision to see how this report fits in with everything else she knows.

In her thoughts, she might imagine the report being read to her. At the same time, Mary might be visualizing what the report will mean in practice for the future of her company.

Exercise

Again, think of someone who is excellent at this type of activity. What is the person's physiology like when he is engaged in this activity? What do you imagine his emotional state is like? Where is he placing his sensory attention? What he is thinking and, more importantly, how he is thinking when he does this.

For each step, anchor these pieces of the BEAT, either kinesthetically using your fingers or spatially using steps toward your desk or four areas of your office space.

Taking Her Mentee to Lunch

If Mary approaches this lunch in the fiery and inspirational way that she spoke to the group in the morning, her poor mentee may be overwhelmed. If she speaks to her in the same way that she dealt with the report, her mentee will feel that she is cold and distant.

Exercise

Have you ever been to lunch with someone you really care about? What is your physiology like when you do? How are you feeling when you listen to the person and offer him your counsel? Are you paying exquisite attention to how the person looks and to his tone of voice as he speaks?

Perhaps this is the way for Mary to be...

Taking Her Client to Dinner

The appropriate BEAT for this will depend upon the relationship Mary has with the client. Perhaps her physiology will be open, leaning back in her chair with hands showing open gestures. She is probably smiling and nodding.

Her emotional state might be one of friendship and sharing.

Her attention will be wrapped around the client. See the discussion of the coaching state in Chapter 14 for details on how this can be done.

Mary may be visualizing the client telling her how happy he is with her company's services.

Conclusion

It is well worth the time and effort to create and install one or more BEAT Systems that you will find useful in your professional life, such as those discussed above.

If you aren't sure of your ability to create any of these BEAT Systems, a great first step is to think about somebody you know who is excellent at that and copy him or her. (You can read more on modeling others in the book *Deep Trance Identification* by Shawn Carson and Jess Marion with John Overdurf.)

Chapter 20: The Acting BEAT

In this chapter, we will talk about how you can use the structure of the BEAT System to instantly enter into the state of your character using the principles of Stanislavski.

Stanislavski created a complete guide for acting, called "method acting." A complete discussion of this method is outside the scope of this short chapter. All we can do is to show you how to take a few of the elements of Stanislavski's method and build them into the BEAT. What this will do is to allow any budding actors out there to quickly and easily step into their role using the BEAT System.

Using the Physical Body in Stanislavski's Method

Stanislavski spent a good deal of time talking about how to use the physical body, including the voice. Students were given specific training in using their bodies to present the character of their role.

Interestingly, Stanislavski reversed the order (of importance) of the four elements of the BEAT. So whereas the BEAT places the body and physiology first and the thoughts last, Stanislavski very clearly placed imagination (thoughts) first and use of the body last. Why is this? It's because most classical systems for training the entire person recognize that where the mind goes first, the emotional energy and body follow. In Eastern traditions, this is often stated as "mind first, energy follows."

This is undoubtedly true, and yet the other side of the coin is that it's often much easier to control your body than your mind. This is especially true if you are upset, as your mind is running "a mile a minute" with negative thoughts. It's easy to shift your physiology, even if you're not in a positive emotional state and aren't thinking great thoughts. You can still straighten and align your spine, balance your weight evenly between your feet, deepen your breathing, and so on. And when you do shift your physiology, it has an immediate and direct impact on your emotional state.

So using your imagination to see the world as you want it to be—or in the case of acting, as your character sees the world—is the most direct way of achieving your goals. But the easiest way to change your state from negative to positive is by using your body and your physiology.

Therefore, using the BEAT System in the way we have described—leading with the body and the physiology—is most likely to be beneficial for any actor who may be experiencing a little stage fright!

Stanislavski's Emotion Memory

Stanislavski warned his students against learning rote actions. He said that simply behaving as you think your character should behave would come across to the audience as insincere and contrived.

Instead, Stanislavski advised students to use the "emotion memory" to remember the feelings associated with the scene. When an actor uses his emotion memory to begin to feel the emotions of his character in a scene, his actions can arise out of those emotions. When the actions arise out of his true emotions, the audience will believe in his character and the scene.

Stanislavski used imagination to recreate these emotions and trigger the emotion memory. He advised his students to think back to some past events in their own lives when they experienced similar emotions, fully step back into those memories, and reexperience those emotions. This is a great way to get in touch with specific emotions and is a great tool for building a "memory palace" of emotions based upon events from your own life.

Of course, you can then anchor these emotions using spatial, kinesthetic, or other types of anchors, as discussed in Chapter 4.

Stanislavski's Spotlight of Attention

Stanislavski was particularly concerned about where the actor placed his attention.

On the most basic level, this means whether the actor is paying attention to the scene around him or the audience. Stanislavski used the metaphor of a couple who are sitting alone in a hotel room when suddenly a large door opens and they see a number of their neighbors staring at them. Obviously, the dynamic of their interaction would change entirely. This is similar to what may happen if the actor's attention moves from the scene on the stage to the audience.

Once the actor's attention is properly on the stage, the question still remains as to where on the stage it should be. This is obviously a matter for the playwright, director, and actor; by writing the scene, the playwright defines the overall point of attention within the scene, the director interprets the scene to provide specific direction to the actor's attention, and the actor interprets the character within the director's direction.

Stanislavski's approach used a mental spotlight to direct the actor's attention. The actor would imagine a spotlight moving around the stage, and his attention would follow the spotlight. In fact, Stanislavski would actually use a real spotlight in the first instance to show the actor where to place his attention. This spotlight acted as a sort of spatial anchor until the actor became conditioned to place his attention in that direction.

Stanislavski's "IF"

The starting point for Stanislavski's work was imagination. According to him, the whole foundation of acting was to act "as if" the actor was the character and the character's world was the actor's world. This was achieved using the actor's imagination—that is to say, using the power of thought. This use of the imagination created belief and a sense of truth in the actors.

Stanislavski described this as "transferring the life of the imagination onto the stage and creating fictitious events of your own, similar to reality."

Putting the BEAT System Together for Acting

The BEAT for acting is no different from any other version of the BEAT.

The first step, perhaps, is to choose four appropriate anchors. These could be four steps that you take to enter the stage. Or they could be four kinesthetic anchors, as long as you can fire them off and still stay in character!

In any case, once you have your four anchors chosen, you simply need to set up the four elements of the BEAT:

Step 1: Body and Breathing, "B"

Rather than stepping into your own peak state, you will be stepping into the state of your character. For this purpose, you need to have a very clear visual image of what your character looks like, including his or her physiology and posture, facial expression, gestures, breathing, and so on.

Once you have that picture, see your character in front of you, life-size and three-dimensional. Imagine stepping or floating into that character, and feel your own physiology change to match his or hers. As you do so, fire off the first anchor.

Repeat this step until the anchor is conditioned.

Step 2: Emotions, "E"

Using Stanislavski's technique, first think about what emotion your character is feeling. To identify this emotion can be an exercise in itself! Once you have this emotion, think back to a time in your life when you felt a similar emotion. Float back into that memory, see what you're seeing, hear what you're hearing, and begin to feel what you're feeling.

Really get in touch with that feeling, notice where in your body it arises, where and how it moves, and whether it has a size or color or vibration or temperature. As you feel the emotion in your body, fire off the second anchor.

Repeat this step until the anchor is conditioned.

Step 3: Awareness, "A"

While you are onstage, or while you are imagining the stage, create your own "spotlight of the imagination." This spotlight will move around the people or objects on the stage to show you exactly where you should be placing your attention. If you're working with the director, the director may tell you where this should be.

Also be aware of the quality of your attention. Are you focusing on one small part of the stage, or is your attention more diffuse? You can begin to condition this by imagining that the spotlight is either very focused or more diffuse and covering more of the stage.

As you begin to track this spotlight of the imagination around the stage and sense the appropriate level and style of attention, fire off the third anchor.

Repeat this step to condition the third anchor.

Step 4: Thoughts, "T"

Now begin to use your imagination to create the reality, the "IF" of your character. In your imagination, you can see your character's backstory—how he or she came to be in this specific time and place. And you can also see your character's goals and outcomes—what he or she wants to achieve from the interaction onstage. These goals may be immediate or more long-term.

In any case, use your imagination to construct the sweep of your character's life from past through to the present scene and into the future. As you do so, fire off the fourth anchor.

Repeat this step to condition the fourth anchor.

Putting It All Together

Now that all your four anchors are set and conditioned, you can begin to chain them together into the BEAT System for this particular character in this particular scene. Please be aware that you may need to build a different BEAT System for different scenes in the same play because your character may have different emotional states, will certainly be paying attention to different parts of the stage, and will also have a different outcome for each scene, even if his or her larger outcomes are similar.

As you take those four steps onto the stage, or as you begin to fire off the kinesthetic anchors, or as you think B-E-A-T, allow your physiology to change to become your character, your emotions to adopt the emotions of the character, your attention to begin to track the spotlight of your imagination, and the sweep of your character from past through to the current scene and into the future to be created in your imagination.

Make any adjustments to any of the steps needed based on your own analysis and feelings, or the direction of the director, or the feedback, as appropriate.

Chapter 21: The Sports BEAT

The sports BEAT is a little different from the other BEAT Systems we have described. In particular, the ordering of the steps is typically different, steps may be repeated a number of times, and the anchoring is done in a different way.

The easiest time to see the sports BEAT in practice is in sports in which the player has the opportunity to prepare for a specific play, such as a golfer on the tee or a baseball batter at the plate.

While each sport, and each player, will be slightly different, you will see sufficient commonalities to be able to decipher their unique BEAT.

In this chapter, we will present a generic sports BEAT that you can use as the basis for developing your own specific style.

Before we describe the sports BEAT in detail, we will go through some of the differences between the sports BEAT and other BEAT Systems.

Initial Gateway Anchor

Many athletes have a ritual or routine they go through before they even step forward to participate in their sport.

You can think of this ritual or routine as a "gateway" leading from their everyday state into the place where they can access their peak sports state. This is not to say that they are necessarily stepping into their peak state at that point in time—more that they are leaving behind any thoughts or emotions that are inconsistent with that peak state.

Some players may simply take a deep breath, others may say a short prayer, and still others may simply pick up the ball or bat. Sometimes these rituals are fairly obvious, such as sumo wrestlers carrying out their ritual dance called the Chirichozu prior to a bout or the New Zealand rugby team doing the traditional Maori haka before a match, but sometimes these rituals can be very personal and may be very subtle and difficult to see.

Sometimes these rituals are fairly bizarre, such as growing a beard prior to a major sporting event. Rumor has it that this ritual was started by the famous Swedish tennis player Bjorn Borg, who used to grow a beard prior to his appearances at Wimbledon. This ritual has been adopted by a number of athletes, especially in the United States. Growing a beard tells the unconscious mind that it is time to focus all one's attention on the sport.

Anchoring Using Sport-Specific Actions

One difference between the sports BEAT and other BEAT Systems is that in the sports BEAT, the physical actions of the sport often become the anchor for the various parts of the BEAT experience. A great way to see this is on the golf course as a player gets ready to tee off. Here you will see the golfer begin graceful practice swings before addressing the ball. You will see the same pattern in baseball; as the batter approaches the plate, he will typically stop a few feet away and take some easy swings with his bat. Note that this action is not intended to warm up his body, as he has already warmed up before stepping up to the plate. Rather, the swinging of the bat acts as an anchor to begin to put his mind and emotions in an appropriate place.

Other examples of using sport-specific actions as anchors for the player's emotional and mental state include a tennis player bouncing the ball prior to his serve, a baseball pitcher taking the ball in his hand, and so on.

Reordering the Steps of the Sports BEAT

When playing a particular sport, the body has been used in a very specific way. For this reason, the body, "B," is typically set as the very last step of the pattern.

However, prior to this final setting of the body in the ideal stance for the sport, various other physical shifts might take place, such as loosening the body, setting the self relative to the ball or other spatial landmark, and so on.

In other words, the body is set into its ideal state in an incremental way, perhaps something like this:
- Relaxing the body
- Taking the stance
- Setting the body

Let's take an example of a specific sports BEAT. In honor of the recently retired New York Yankees superstar Derek Jeter, we will look at his BEAT pattern as he steps up to the plate to bat.

Jeter begins his BEAT with a gateway ritual. He squats down on his haunches as if in prayer or meditation, clearing his mind for what is to come. He then takes his bat and rubs the handle to prepare it.

Having prepared both his mind and his bat, Jeter now steps toward the plate but stops a few feet away. He begins to swing the bat in an easy rhythm, settling both his mind and emotions into the peak state.

Jeter now steps to the plate. He puts his right foot in place and reaches his bat toward the plate to measure the distance as he is settling his left foot.

Jeter will likely glance up at the pitcher for a moment, then look down at the ground, and perhaps go inside for a moment to ensure that his mind and emotions are still set.

He turns his eyes toward the pitcher, his gaze taking in all possible paths of the ball.

He now sets the rest of his body in his batting stance, gently encircling his bat as he does so… Ready to face the pitch.

The Sports BEAT

Here are the steps of the sports BEAT. Take these only as a guide and modify them for your own sport and your own style. You may want to develop a few different sports BEATs for different stages of your sport.

Step 1: Gateway Ritual

Choose or develop a ritual that will tell your unconscious mind that you are about to engage in your sport. Practice this ritual until it is second nature, putting your attention on entering into a calm state each time you practice. The state does not need to be your peak performance state (yet), but it does need to be clear of any distractions that could otherwise impact your performance.

Step 2: Sport-Specific Movement as an Anchor for Thoughts

Choose some movement that is specific to your sport. It may be something obvious like swinging a bat, or something subtler such as squeezing your fist if you are a martial artist. This will act as the anchor for your thoughts and emotions. Begin to imagine performing your sport perfectly—throwing the ideal pitch, strongly striking a ball, making a pass, or whatever it might be. As you imagine this strongly in your mind's eye, perform the action so that this thought becomes anchored to the action.

Step 3: Sport-Specific Movement as an Anchor for Emotions

Repeat the second step, this time focusing on the emotional state you will need in order to perform your sport perfectly.

Repeat the second and third steps until each time you perform the action, you have the mental image of performing your sport perfectly as well as the associated emotional state.

Step 4: Taking Your Stance

Step onto the playing area and take your playing stance, whatever that might be. You will want to set one foot first and then the other. In many sports, your stance will be set relative to something else—the ball in golf, the free throw line in basketball, the plate in baseball, and so on. Always set your stance in the same way, for example, starting with the same foot and measuring distance in the same way. In this way, setting your stance also becomes a ritual that can lead you deeper into your peak state. Practice even this small action until it becomes automatic.

Step 5: Checking Your Emotional State

Now that you have set your stance, take a moment to go inside and recalibrate your thoughts and emotional state. Typically the easiest time to do this is while you are looking down. Check to make sure that your thoughts and emotional state are still ideal and are supportive of your peak state. The time to get this right is when you're practicing so that when you are actually competing, all of this becomes second nature.

Step 6: Viewing the Field

Lift up your eyes and observe the field. Your field of view should take in everything that is relevant while eliminating everything that is irrelevant and perhaps distracting. So, for example, if you are playing basketball, typically everything on the court is going to be relevant, and everything off the court, such as the spectators, irrelevant. If you are boxing, your field of vision should be taking in your entire opponent from head to foot and fist to fist, as well as an awareness of the location of the ropes. If you are a golfer, your awareness may be much more centered on the golf ball as you swing.

A great example of this focused awareness can be seen in the movie *The Legend of Bagger Vance*. In this movie, Will Smith is a mystical golf caddie named Bagger Vance who teaches a golfer, Rannulph Junuh (played by Matt Damon), the secrets of inner golf. In one scene, Bagger Vance teaches Junuh how to "see the field." When Junuh does this, his gaze takes in the fairway, the green appears to be much closer than before, and the spectators disappear. Once more, the key is to take in everything that is important to the sport while allowing everything else to fade into the background.

Step 7: Setting the Body

Now allow your body to set itself in the ideal physical state for your sport. Exactly what this is will vary from sport to sport, particularly in regard to the position of the torso, the position of the arms and hands, the position of the head, and so on.

As noted above, the sports BEAT can be very specific to a particular sport as well as the individual athlete. It can also be specific to the situation within the game. For example, a baseball player may have one BEAT when he is stepping up to the plate, a second BEAT when on base, and a third BEAT when in the field. Be flexible.

The key to the sports BEAT is to practice, practice, practice. By the time you actually get to a competition, you need to be able to step into your peak states quickly and easily by virtue of the ten thousand repetitions of all the BEAT Systems you have done in practice.

Chapter 22: Musashi's Samurai BEAT

Musashi Miyamoto is without a doubt the most famous Japanese samurai of all time.

Orphaned at the age of seven, Musashi became a ronin—a masterless samurai who dedicated his life to studying the art of the sword. From the age of thirteen until the age of twenty-nine, Musashi fought more than sixty duels with other samurai, defeating them all. He fought his first duel at the age of thirteen against a fully armed, expert samurai warrior. His unfortunate opponent was unceremoniously thrown to the ground by Musashi and beaten about the head with a stick until he died.

Musashi retired from dueling at age twenty-nine but continued to study the way of the sword. In fact, Musashi claimed he did not learn kendo until after the age of thirty! In his later years, Musashi set down his fighting system in a series of five short books, which he called *The Book of Five Rings*.

The second of these is called *The Water Book*, and in this book Musashi describes what he calls the spirit or principles of sword fighting and describes his version of the BEAT System. This is the first explicit description of a BEAT System that we have found anywhere.

We are going to take Musashi's description and realign it just a little with the four steps of the BEAT that we have become familiar with.

Step 1: Body

Musashi spends a good deal of time describing his ideal physiology for sword fighting. You might want to stand up and follow along as we run through his description:

- Your head should be erect, not looking down or looking up, and not twisted. Your forehead and the space between your eyes are relaxed, with no frown or furrows. Your face is composed. Musashi describes how you should slightly flare your nostrils.
- Your eyes should be slightly narrowed.
- You should feel energy throughout your body, your shoulders should be pulled slightly down, and your abdomen should be firm.
- Your buttocks should be pulled in, and you should put strength into your legs from the knees to the toes.

Musashi also describes how you should hold a sword, putting strength into the last two fingers of the hand, with the middle finger and the thumb and index finger "floating." Unless you are actually planning on using a sword, this may be too much information!

Musashi describes the ideal way of walking, with firm weight on the heels and "floating" toes.

Step 2: Emotions

Musashi also addresses the emotional state of a samurai warrior, which he refers to as the "spirit." The warrior should maintain a state of calm rather than being emotional or reckless. However, this is not a state of relaxation but rather a point of equilibrium between relaxation and tension that Musashi describes as "neither insufficiently spirited nor over spirited."

Musashi also describes this as a state that you should maintain throughout your life, not just in combat. He also points out that your emotional state should be independent of your physical state so that even if your body is relaxed, your spirit maintains a certain level of arousal. Also, if your spirit is relaxed in battle, you do not allow this to make your body more relaxed than it should be.

Finally, he warns against allowing your opponent to see your spirit. Whatever emotions you are feeling, you should present a state of calm to the world around you while in battle.

Step 3: Awareness

Musashi is very specific about your gaze and sensory awareness. On reading his description, it very much sounds like a description of peripheral vision or the coaching state! He describes the difference between foveal vision and peripheral vision in a number of interesting and quite poetic ways.

Firstly, Musashi says that the gaze should be "broad," allowing the warrior to look to both sides without moving his eyeballs (peripheral vision).

He describes the twofold gaze of "perception and sight." He also says that it is important to see distant things as if they were close, and close things as if they were distant. This allows you to be aware of your opponent's sword without being distracted by its movement.

Step 4: Thoughts

Finally Musashi moves on to thoughts. What thoughts should a warrior have in battle? Musashi is very clear on this point: the samurai thinks only of "cutting his enemy." With this single thought in mind, the body acts naturally to wield the sword in the most efficient way.

Applying the Warrior BEAT in Everyday Life

The BEAT described by Musashi in *The Book of Five Rings* is very similar to many of the BEAT applications we have described:

- Hold your body in an erect and balanced way with your physical attention on your abdomen.
- Use a balanced emotional state, one that allows you to act forcefully when necessary while remaining calm and reserved.
- Open up your sight in particular, and your senses in general, to take in all relevant information, even information that you did not know was relevant until it appeared.
- Put your thoughts entirely on your outcome—what you want to achieve in the moment. When you're in the midst of battle, it is too late to plan—it's time to act.

The beauty of reading Musashi's description of the samurai BEAT is that it puts this wonderful system in a deep historical tradition. If you're truly invested in achieving great things in your life, perhaps you occasionally need to step into the role of the greatest-ever samurai!

Conclusion

As we come to the end of our exploration of the BEAT System, you are ready to step into your future, filled with the confidence that your newfound skills will allow you to meet any challenge, see the world through new eyes, and know that you have the ability to be whoever you want to be.

We have two selves in time: a present self and a self that lives in the past (through memories) and in the future (through planning and daydreaming). Having said this, everything that we do—everything that we actually achieve in life—is actually done in the moment. Even our plans are made in the moment. By having instant and total control over your physical actions, your emotional state, your awareness of the world, and your thoughts, you can achieve more than you ever thought possible.

Imagine, if you will, that your ideal future self—the future self who has truly mastered the BEAT System—is standing in front of you. What would you see when you look at that future "you"—what lets you know you have achieved this mastery? Now imagine stepping forward into the future "you" and feeling that mastery at your fingertips, secure in the knowledge that it feels as if it's woven into your bones.

Notice how you'll be feeling now that you have this mastery at your fingertips. It gives you confidence to know that you can feel amazing and step into your ideal state at any time and in any situation. In fact, step into that ideal state right now and feel how good it feels.

Now that you have that total sense of confidence, knowing those skills are at your fingertips, you can see the world in a new way. It is transformed from a struggle to a challenge— a challenge that you're able to see your way through (or over, or around). Seeing the world in this way makes all the difference.

In fact, all you have to do now is begin to imagine that your goal—your outcome—is within reach. You can see yourself meeting and overcoming any challenges and easily reaching this goal.

The power of the BEAT System is limited only by your imagination. Any skill—physical, emotional, sensory, or intellectual—can be woven into your own individual BEAT System. You can perform at your best each and every minute of each and every day, beginning right now.

Other Books In This Series

The Swish
By Shawn Carson and Jess Marion

The Visual Squash
By Jess Marion and Shawn Carson

The Meta Pattern
By Shawn and Sarah Carson

Other Books By This Publisher

Deep Trance Identification: Unconscious Modeling and Mastery for Hypnosis Practitioners, Coaches, and Everyday People
By Shawn Carson and Jess Marion with John Overdurf

Quit: The Hypnotist's Handbook to Running Effective Stop Smoking Sessions
By Jess Marion, Sarah Carson, and Shawn Carson

Keeping the Brain in Mind: Practical Neuroscience for Coaches, Therapists, and Hypnosis Practitioners
By Shawn Carson and Melissa Tiers

Tree of Life Coaching: Practical Secrets of the Kabbalah for Hypnosis and NLP Practitioners and Coaches
By Shawn Carson

I Quit: Stop Smoking Easily Through the Power of Hypnosis
By Jess Marion, Sarah Carson, and Shawn Carson

www.ingramcontent.com/pod-product-compliance
Lightning Source LLC
Chambersburg PA
CBHW072003090426
42740CB00011B/2074